State Trooper

State Trooper

Edited by

*Hy Hammer, Chief of
Examining Service Division
New York City Department
of Personnel, (Ret.)*

**ARCO PUBLISHING, INC.
NEW YORK**

Eighth Edition, First Printing, 1984

Published by Arco Publishing, Inc.
215 Park Avenue South, New York, N.Y. 10003

Copyright © 1984 by Arco Publishing, Inc.

Library of Congress Cataloging in Publication Data

Hammer, Hy.
  State trooper.

  Rev. ed. of: State trooper, highway patrolman,
ranger. 7th ed. 1981.
  Includes index.
  1. Police, State—United States —Handbooks, manuals
etc.   I. Hammer, Hy. State trooper, highway patrolman,
ranger.   II. Title.
HV8143.H327   1984   363.2'076   83-15906
ISBN 0-668-05765-3 (pbk.)

Printed in the United States of America

CONTENTS

WHAT THIS BOOK WILL DO FOR YOU

ARCO Publishing, Inc. has followed testing trends and methods ever since the firm was founded in 1937. We specialize in books that prepare people for tests. Based on this experience, we have prepared the best possible book to help *you* score high.

To write this book we carefully analyzed every detail surrounding the forthcoming examination . . .
- the job itself
- official and unofficial announcements concerning the examination
- all the previous examinations, many not available to the public
- related examinations
- technical literature that explains and forecasts the examination

CAN YOU PREPARE YOURSELF FOR YOUR TEST?

You want to pass this test. That's why you bought this book. Used correctly, your "self-tutor" will show you what to expect and will give you a speedy brush-up on the subjects tested in your exam. Some of these are subjects not taught in schools at all. Even if your study time is very limited, you should:

- Become familiar with the type of examination you will have.
- Improve your general examination-taking skill.
- Improve your skill in analyzing and answering questions involving reasoning, judgment, comparison, and evaluation.

- Improve your speed and skill in reading and understanding what you read—an important part of your ability to learn and an important part of most tests.

This book will tell you exactly what to study by presenting in full every type of question you will get on the actual test.

This book will help you find your weaknesses. Once you know what subjects you're weak in you can get right to work and concentrate on those areas. This kind of selective study yields maximum test results.

This book will give you the *feel* of the exam. Almost all our sample and practice questions are taken from actual previous exams. On the day of the exam you'll see how closely this book follows the format of the real test.

This book will give you confidence *now,* while you are preparing for the test. It will build your self-confidence as you proceed and will prevent the kind of test anxiety that causes low test scores.

This book stresses the multiple-choice type of question because that's the kind you'll have on your test. You must not be satisfied with merely knowing the correct answer for each question. You must find out why the other choices are incorrect. This will help you remember a lot you thought you had forgotten.

After testing yourself, you may find that you are weak in a particular area. You should concentrate on improving your skills by using the specific practice sections in this book that apply to you.

1

PART ONE

Applying For Your Job

The examination to be taken by State Trooper candidates varies from state to state. The examiners are always intent on determining the applicant's learning ability. They also try to determine how well the applicant will be able to react to the various demands of the job.

The Sample Examinations in this book draw upon the types of questions found in examinations of many states. Not all examinations use all kinds of questions and some states might present a unique question style. Thorough study of this book, with careful attention to the Sample Examinations, will prepare you for the most common types of questions. You may determine the specific varieties of test questions you will face by carefully studying the examination announcement of your own state.

APPLYING FOR STATE JOBS

JOB OPENINGS

State employment opportunities cover practically every skill and profession in our complex modern social order. Every year thousands of new jobs are created and tens of thousands of replacements are needed on existing jobs.

Most state commissions have recruitment procedures for filling civil service positions. They have developed a number of methods to make job opportunities known. Places where such information may be obtained include:

1. Your state Civil Service Commission. Address your inquiry to the capital city of your state.

2. The offices of the State Employment Services. There are almost two thousand throughout the country. These offices are administered by the state in which they are located, with the financial assistance of the Federal government. You will find the address of the one nearest you in your telephone book.

3. Your municipal building and your local library.

4. Complete listings are carried by *The Chief* and other city and state-wide publications devoted to Civil Service employees. Many local newspapers run a section on regional civil service news.

5. State and local agencies looking for competent employees will contact schools, professional societies, veterans organizations, unions, and trade associations.

While regular civil service appointments are made by the Department of Civil Service of your state, there are also temporary and provisional jobs to be had from other state agencies. If you are interested in such appointments a few minutes with the telephone book will give you a list of such agencies in your state.

The Job Announcement

WHAT IT CONTAINS

When a position is open and a civil service examination is to be given for it, a job announcement is drawn up. This generally contains just about everything an applicant has to know about the job.

The announcement begins with the job title and salary. A typical announcement then describes the work, the location of the position, the education and experience requirements, the kind of examination to be given, the system of rating. It may also have something to say about veteran preference and the age limit. It tells which application form is to be filled out, where to get the form, and where and when to file it.

Study the job announcement carefully. It will answer many of your questions and help you decide whether you like the position and are qualified for it.

WHERE THE JOB IS LOCATED

If the job is a state job, be sure you are willing to work in the area indicated. There is no point in applying for a position and taking the examination if you do not want to move. If you are not willing to move, study other announcements that will give you an opportunity to work in a place of your choice.

A civil service job close to your home has as an additional advantage the fact that local residents usually receive preference in appointments.

THE DUTIES

The words *Optional Fields*—sometimes just the word *Options*—may appear on the front page of the announcement. You then have a choice to apply for that particular position in which you are especially interested. This is because the duties of various positions are quite different even though they bear the same broad title. A public relations *clerk*, for example, does different work from a payroll *clerk*, although they are considered broadly in the same general area.

Not every announcement has options. But whether or not it has them, the precise duties are described in detail, usually under the heading: *Description of Work*. Make sure that these duties come within the range of your experience and ability.

THE DEADLINE

Most job requirements give a deadline for filing an application. Others bear the words, *No Closing Date*, at the top of the first page; this means that applications will be accepted until the needs of the agency are met. In some cases a public notice is issued when a certain number of applications have been received.

No application mailed past the deadline date will be considered.

EDUCATION AND EXPERIENCE

Every announcement has a detailed section on education and experience requirements for the particular job and for the optional fields. Make sure that in both education and experience you meet the minimum qualifications. If you do not meet the given standards for one job, there may be others open where you stand a better chance of making the grade.

VETERAN PREFERENCE

If the job announcement does not mention veteran preference, it would be wise to inquire if there is such a provision in your state or municipality. There may be none or it may be limited to disabled veterans. In some jurisdictions widows of veterans are given preference. All such information can be obtained through the agency that issues the job announcement.

WHY YOU MAY BE BARRED

Applicants may be denied examinations and eligibles may be denied appointments for any of the following reasons:

—intentional false statements;

—deception or fraud in examination or appointment;

—reasonable doubt concerning loyalty to the United States;

—use of intoxicating beverages to excess;

—criminal, infamous, dishonest, immoral, or notoriously disgraceful conduct.

THE TEST

The announcement describes the kind of test given for the particular position. Please pay special attention to this section. It tells what areas are to be covered in the written test and lists the specific subjects on which questions will be asked. Sometimes sample questions are given.

The test and review material in this Arco book are based on the requirements as given in this section as well as on actual tests.

Usually the announcement states whether the examination is to be assembled or unassembled. In an *assembled* examination applicants *assemble* in the same place at the same time to take a written or performance test. The unassembled examination is one where an applicant does not take a test; instead the applicant is rated on education and experience and whatever records of past achievement he or she is asked to provide.

HOW TO GET AN APPLICATION FORM

Having studied the job announcement and having decided that you want the position and are qualified for it, your next step is to get an application form. The job announcement tells you where to send for it.

The Application Form

On the whole, civil service application forms differ little from state to state and locality to locality. The questions, which have been worked out after years of experimentation, are simple and direct, designed to elicit a maximum of information about you.

Many prospective civil service employees have failed to get a job because of slipshod, erroneous, incomplete, misleading, or untruthful answers. Give the application the serious attention it must have as the first important step toward getting the job you want.

Here, along with some helpful comments, are the questions usually asked on the average application form, although not necessarily in this order.

THE QUESTIONS

Name of examination or kind of position applied for. This information appears in large type on the first page of the job announcement.

Optional job (if mentioned in the announcement). If you wish to apply for an option, simply copy the title from the announcement. If you are not interested in an option, write "None."

Primary place of employment applied for. This would pertain to a state-wide job. The location of the position was probably contained in the announcement. You must consider whether you want to work there. The announcement may list more than one location where the job is open. If you would accept employment in any of the places, list them all; otherwise list the specific place or places where you would be willing to work.

Name and Address. Give in full, including your middle name if you have one, and your maiden name as well if you are a married woman.

Home and Office phones. If none, write "None."

Legal or voting residence. The state in which you vote is the one you list here.

Married or single. If you are a widow or widower, you are considered single.

Birthplace. Changes in the borders of European countries make it difficult for many foreign-born American citizens to know which country to list as the land of their birth. One suggestion is to set down the name of the town and the name of the country which now controls it, together with the name of the country to which it belonged at the time of your birth.

Date of birth. Give the exact day, month, and year.

Lowest grade or pay you will accept. Although the salary is clearly stated in the job announcement, there may be a quicker opening in the same occupation but carrying less responsibility and thus a lower basic entrance salary. You will not be considered for a job paying less than the amount you give in answer to this question.

Will you accept temporary employment if offered you for (a) one month or less, (b) one to four months, (c) four to twelve months? Temporary positions come up frequently and it is important to know whether you are available.

Will you accept less than full-time employment? Part-time work comes up now and then. Consider whether you want to accept such a position while waiting for a full-time appointment.

Were you in active military service in the Armed Forces of the United States? Veterans' preference, if given, is usually limited to active service during the following periods: December 7, 1941 to September 2, 1945; June 26, 1950 to July 27, 1953; January 1, 1963 to May 7, 1975.

Do you claim disabled veterans credit? If you do, you have to show proof of a war-incurred disability. This is done through certification by the Veterans Administration.

Considerable space is allotted on the form for the applicant to tell about all his past employment. Examiners check all such answers closely. DO NOT embroider or falsify your record. If you were ever fired, say so. It is better for you to state this openly than for the examiners to find out the truth from your former employer.

Special qualifications and skills. Even though not directly related to the position for which you are applying, such information as licenses and certificates obtained for teacher, pilot, registered nurses, and so on is wanted. Also, experience in the use of machines and equipment, and a list of whatever other skills you have acquired. Also, published writings, public speaking experience, membership in professional societies, honors and fellowships received.

Education. List your entire educational history, including all diplomas degrees, special courses taken in any accredited or Armed Forces school. Also give your credits toward a college or a graduate degree.

References. The names of people who can give information about you, with their occupations and business and home addresses, are often requested.

Your health. Questions are asked concerning your medical record. You are expected to have the physical and psychological capacity to perform the job for which you are applying. Standards vary, of course, depending on the requirements of the position. Physical handicaps will not bar applicants from jobs they can perform adequately.

THE EXAMINATIONS

When you have filled out the application as completely as possible, sign it and send it to the address given on the form. If your examination includes a written test, you must wait until it is scheduled. Shortly before it is to be held, you will be notified where and when to report.

YOU ARE TESTED

Sometimes the date of the written test appears on the job announcement. Sometimes it does not and you must simply wait until you receive notification of the time and place.

The period between the filing of the application and the taking of the test can be of immense value to you. If you use it wisely, it will help you score high.

The most important step you can take in preparing for your test is to study questions on previous tests—or questions similar to those asked on previous tests. The purpose of this book is to acquaint you with the kinds of questions that will be asked and to provide you with review material in the subjects that will be covered. A thorough knowledge of the forms of the actual test as well as of the subject matter will give you a great advantage. There are no substitutes for experience and familiarity.

THE DAY OF THE TEST

The importance of knowing beforehand exactly how to reach the test center and how to get there cannot be stressed enough. Lateness will bar you from taking the test. There is nothing more nerve-wracking than to find yourself in a traffic jam and on the wrong bus with little time to spare. If the test is to take place some distance from your house, make the trip a few days earlier to make sure you know how to get there. On the all-important day give yourself more than enough time. In this way you will avoid the risk of an upsetting experience under circumstances that may affect your final score.

THE ELIGIBLE LIST

When all the parts of the examination have been rated (this may include education, experience, and suitability along with the written test), you are notified of your *numerical* rating. If this is high enough to give you a passing mark, you are placed on the eligible list. Appointments are made from this list.

SAMPLE OFFICIAL ANNOUNCEMENTS

STATE TROOPER

JOB ELEMENTS To perform the duties of a State Trooper you must have good judgment, thoroughness, conscientiousness, common sense, motivation and enthusiasm for the job. You must be dependable and willing to get involved. You must be able to assume responsibility; make decisions often under pressure; work without supervision; take orders; function in physical danger; act under pressure; communicate well; and combine physical and mental resources.

DUTIES AND RESPONSIBILITIES As a State Trooper, you will use these characteristics to perform duties involving patrol, investigation, station duties, maintenance activities and special assignments:

*In the course of your *patrol duties* you will direct traffic, assist lost, stranded, or disabled motorists, approach motorists on routine or non–routine violations and make arrests. You may be called upon to control crowds and support other Troopers in stress situations. Other patrol duties will include inspecting and safeguarding property, responding to bank alarms, chasing violators on foot and checking buildings at night for break–ins.

*When you perform *investigative duties* your work will include interviewing complainants and witnesses, aiding people injured in highway, home and industrial accidents, handling fatal accident and crime scenes, responding to complaints involving vicious animals, using deadly physical force or firearms, interrogating suspects and executing search and arrest warrants.

*There are times when you will be expected to carry out *desk work*. You will send and receive radio and teletype messages, make entries in station records, respond to telephone inquiries concerning weather and road conditions, locations, law or other topics. You will also prepare written memoranda and reports.

*You will be required to maintain a good *personal appearance*. Your equipment, uniforms and vehicle must be properly cared for. You also will assist in keeping your station clean and orderly.

*In the course of your career, you may be assigned to *special work*. These assignments may be varied and may include securing major disaster areas, policing areas during natural disasters, participating in community public relations programs, escorting V.I.P.'s, presenting speeches or lectures, scuba diving, recruit training or counseling. When the work schedule or special duty requires it, you will work on weekends, holidays, irregular hours, overtime and in inclement weather.

HOW TO APPLY Application blanks are available at all State Police Stations. Candidates may also obtain the forms in person or by mail. You *must* file a completed written application in order to be eligible to take the written examination. You will then be advised of the time and place of the written examination and provided with an admission ticket to the test location most convenient to you.

EXAMINATION LOCATIONS The state capital and most large cities. Exact locations can be found on the latest announcements.

GENERAL INFORMATION The number of candidates selected and appointment dates will depend on budget allocations. All appointments are probationary. The list established from this examination will remain in effect for a minimum of one year and maximum of four years. All qualified candidates will receive equal consideration for employment without regard to sex, race, religion, color or national origin.

EXAMINATION PROCEDURES The complete examination procedure for Trooper is based on elements of the job, and will consist of four phases: A WRITTEN EXAMINATION, a PHYSICAL PERFORMANCE TEST, an ORAL INTERVIEW and a BACKGROUND INVESTIGATION OF FITNESS. The selection process will be job—related in content and competitive in nature in order to determine the candidate's potential for performance as a State Trooper. *No prior police experience is required.*

The written examination will be the first phase of Trooper selection. More information concerning the written examination will be provided with the application forms. The 4,000 candidates who score highest on the written examination will qualify for the next phase of the selection process: the physical performance test. This test, which is in two parts, is designed to measure the candidate's ability to combine mental and physical resources. In the first part, the candidate must perform minimal physical tests that will be evaluated on a pass—fail basis. Those passing will be qualified to compete in the second part consisting of additional physical tests which will be competitively scored. Detailed requirements for the performance test, and when it will be given, will be provided to candidates selected to compete in this phase.

A competitive list will then be established of the qualifying candidates in the order of the combined scores achieved on the written examination and the physical performance test, to which will be added allowable Veterans Credit, as claimed. The maximum score on the written phase will be 65; maximum score on the performance phase will be 35.

As new Trooper positions are authorized, the number of candidates needed will be notified to appear for an oral interview. Notifications will be made in the order of rank on the established competitive list. The oral interview will be graded on a pass—fail basis. Those passing will then be eligible for appointment, subject to meeting all administrative requirements and receiving a satisfactory evaluation following a background investigation of fitness.

VETERAN'S PREFERENCE Candidates who are veterans and who qualify on the examination may claim veterans' credit. To claim credits, candidates must have been residents of New York State at the time of entry into the Armed Forces of the U.S., and such service must have been during the period of January 1, 1963 to March 29, 1973. The credit of five points for non-disabled veterans or ten points for disabled veterans is applied only to the final score of passing candidates being placed on the eligible list. Eligible candidates will be furnished with appropriate forms to claim such credit after the written examination phase and will be required to furnish proper documentation.

ADMINISTRATIVE REQUIREMENTS In addition to successfully completing the competitive examinations, a candidate must meet administrative standards established by the Division of State Police:

*Minimum Age – *All candidates must be at least 20 years old on date of examination and at least 21 years old at date of appointment.*

*Maximum Age – Candidates without allowable military service must not have reached their 29th birthday by time of appointment. *Candidates with military duty, as defined in Section 243 of the Military Law, may use allowable service time to extend the age limit proportionately up to a maximum of six years.*

*Education — Candidates must have graduated from a Senior High School or possess a High School Equivalency Diploma *at the time of appointment*. Military GED Certificates must be converted to an equivalency diploma before appointment.

*Residence   Any citizen of the United States is eligible to take the examination. However, New York State law requires that any person appointed as a Trooper must be a resident of this State at the time of appointment and must maintain that residency as long as employment continues.

*Driver's License — Candidates must have a current valid driver's license at the time of appointment.   Candidates must also have a least one year's driving experience.

*Criminal Record – Any felony conviction is an automatic disqualification. Conviction for all other crimes and offenses are subject to evaluation during a background investigation.

*Medical Fitness   Sound health and physical condition are required of all candidates since the physical activities of the job often demand extreme exertion in emergency situations. A medical examination will be given prior to appointment during which vision, hearing, weight, dental condition and general fitness will be determined.

JOB ELEMENT
SELF—APPRAISAL FORM

PLEASE FILL OUT THIS SECTION

NAME (PRINT _____

                    LAST   FIRST   MIDDLE

ADDRESS _____

THIS FORM IS TO BE COMPLETED AND RETURNED WITH YOUR APPLICATION

The Job Element Self-Appraisal Form consists of questions about many of the personal qualities and behaviors which are important in performing the job of a State Trooper. The items have been identified by a thorough study of current job requirements. The information may help you in determining whether you are interested in the job and have some of the needed qualifications.

DIRECTIONS

You are asked to respond to every question on this form in a direct and honest manner. While your answers to this form will not be scored, you should be aware that many of your answers may be checked in later phases of the examination process. For example, requirements in terms of agility and strength will be checked on the Physical Performance Test.

You may not have had the opportunity to do all the job demands listed on this form. On such questions, you will have to make your best judgment as to whether you would be able to meet the demands. If you think that you probably will be able to perform the job demand, give the appropriate answer. On the other hand, if you think you probably won't be able to do so, answer accordingly. When you are doubtful, it may be reasonable to try yourself out on some items before answering them.

JOB ELEMENT
SELF–APPRAISAL FORM
Yes.... No....

1. Do you have the ability to drive:

    (a) on expressways and limited access highways, such as interstate highways, thruways or turnpikes? _____

    (b) in city areas? _____

    (c) in suburban areas? _____

2. Are you able to:

    (a) drive at night for extended periods of time? _____

    (b) drive a car for long periods of time under adverse weather conditions? _____

    (c) quickly transfer your foot from the gas pedal to the brake pedal of a car in an emergency? _____

3. While driving a car, can you move your head from side to side without moving your body? _____

4. If you were driving a full–sized sedan without aids or adaptive devices:

    (a) are you tall enough to see over the steering wheel without assuming a body position that would make safe operation of the car difficult? _____

    (b) could you reach all the hand controls, switches and levers on the dashboard without assuming a body position that would make safe operation of the car difficult? _____

5. Are your legs long enough to reach the gas and brake pedals in a full–sized sedan without the aid of any devices? _____

6. Under normal conditions, do you experience motion sickness while riding in:

    (a) cars? _____

    (b) boats? _____

    (c) planes? _____

7. If you were driving a police car on the way to an emergency, could you maneuver your way through moving traffic using the flashing red lights and siren? _____

8. Are you tall enough to see over the roof of a full–sized sedan (car height approximately 5')? _____

9. Are your arms long enough to hold an Ithaca Model 37 pump–action shotgun level at shoulder height? _____

10. Can you meet these physical requirements:

    (a) climb over a fence four feet high? _____

    (b) hurdle over an obstacle three feet high? _____

    (c) scale a wall four feet high? _____

    (d) climb to the top of a ladder twenty feet high? _____

    (e) enter a window from the top of a ladder? _____

    (f) climb, unaided, into a window five feet above the ground? _____

    (g) climb lengthwise over a full–sized sedan? _____

    (h) pass through an opening three feet by three feet? _____

    (i) pull a 120–lb. object off the road? _____

    (j) lift a 90–lb. weight from ground to waist level and place it in the rear of a station wagon? _____

    (k) change a car tire including removal and tightening of lug nuts from a car wheel? _____

    (l) remove and replace the spare tire from the trunk of a car? _____

    (m) maintain your balance, for example, riding a bicycle? _____

    (n) work without regular meal times? _____

    (o) use a pry bar to force open a car door? _____

11.   (a) Are you missing any fingers, toes, arms or legs? _____

    If you answer "yes," then complete section b of this question.

    (b) If so, so you feel that you could still perform the job of a Trooper? _____

12. Can you accurately copy names, addresses and a long series of numbers and letters as required in filling out a traffic ticket? _____

13. Can you add, subtract, multiply and divide accurately? _____

14. Are you able to copy information accurately from a driver's license and vehicle registration? _____

15. Do you have the mental and physical abilities needed to make an arrest? _____

16. If a police situation required it, could you use a nightstick to poke or hit someone? _____

17. Could you use a gun to kill an injured or vicious animal at close range? _____

18. If you were a Trooper, could you direct traffic? _____

19. In an emergency situation, could you take the responsibility of directing motorists to drive in the wrong traffic lanes or in a direction that they had not intended to drive? _____

20. Can you learn how to use a two–way radio? _____

21.   (a) Are you now or have you been in the military service? _____

    If you answer "yes," then complete section b of this question.

    (b) Are you willing to sign a waiver to permit examination of your military records and/or discharge papers? _____

22. Are you able to:

    (a) run ¼ mile (1,320 feet)? _____

    (b) work outdoors in inclement weather for extended periods of time? _____

23. Do you:

    (a) have sufficient strength in each hand to control a .357 magnum handgun (a powerful weapon with considerable recoil)? _____

    (b) have sufficient strength to control a shotgun during rapid fire? _____

24. Have you had any compensation claims for injury connected with your employment within the past 10 years (including military service)? (If "yes," explain) _____

25. Have you ever been discharged, forced or requested to resign from a job? (If "yes," explain) _____

26. Are you now or have you ever been employed in or compensated for any unlawful activity? (If "yes," explain) _____

27. Do you have:

    (a) frequent and uncontrollable need for sleep? _____

    (b) any speech defects that would interfere with your ability to communicate orally? _____

    (c) any mental or emotional problems that would prevent you from functioning under physical or emotional pressure? _____

    (d) any addiction to unlawful drugs? _____

    (e) any alcohol addiction? _____

    (f) any major physical disabilities? _____

    (g) excessive concern about your health? _____

28. Are you afraid of the dark? _____

29. Are you generally in good health? _____

30. Are you able to maintain your emotional stability without the use of drugs? _____

31. Do you have good peripheral (side) vision? _____

32. Can you focus your eyes quickly on objects at various distances away from you? _____

33. Are you able to distinguish different colors such as in the clothing of suspects and automobiles? _____

34. Can you read a New York State license plate in daylight at a distance of 40 feet? _____

35. Can you move both eyes in the same direction at the same time? _____

36. Can you observe merging traffic while driving? _____

37. When blinded by oncoming headlights at night, are you able to recover from the glare quickly enough to maintain control of your vehicle? _____

38.   (a) Do you wear prescribed glasses? _____

      If you answer "yes," then complete sections b through e of this question.

      If your glasses were broken or removed, could you:

    (b) drive a car? _____

    (c) physically defend yourself in hand to hand combat? _____

    (d) effectively use a handgun at 15 yards? _____

    (e) chase a fleeing person across a field? _____

39. Could you hear and understand a normal radio transmission while on patrol? _____

40. Police officers often have to conduct investigations or make arrests involving members of the opposite sex. Would you be afraid to conduct such investigations or make arrests involving members of the opposite sex? _____

41. Are you willing to:

    (a) physically defend yourself? _____

    (b) inflict physical injury on someone, under proper circumstances, when acting in defense of another person? _____

42. Are you aware of the need for safety when handling firearms? _____

43. Are you afraid to handle or shoot firearms? _____

44. Could you withstand boredom such as driving for a long period at night with no other activity, or watching a specific location for 8 hours without relief? _____

45. Are you honest? _____

46. Can you resist a bribe? _____

47. Can you resist the temptation to accept gratuities, for example, special discounts, free meals? _____

48. Can you distinguish between right and wrong? _____

49. Could you remember your work schedule if the hours were changed from week to week? _____

50. Would you be willing to give up your right to strike in a labor-management dispute as a condition of State Police employment? _____

51. A State Trooper must learn law, legal procedures, interpersonal skills and investigative procedures. Would you be willing to learn:

(a) how to develop information about the criminal elements in a patrol area ⎯⎯⎯⎯⎯⎯⎯⎯⎯

(b) how to make a crime scene search ⎯⎯⎯⎯⎯⎯⎯⎯⎯⎯⎯⎯⎯⎯⎯⎯⎯⎯⎯⎯

(c) how to respond to armed robberies ⎯⎯⎯⎯⎯⎯⎯⎯⎯⎯⎯⎯⎯⎯⎯⎯⎯⎯⎯

(d) the criteria by which evidence is admitted in a trial ⎯⎯⎯⎯⎯⎯⎯⎯⎯⎯⎯⎯⎯

(e) how to plan an investigation ⎯⎯⎯⎯⎯⎯⎯⎯⎯⎯⎯⎯⎯⎯⎯⎯⎯⎯⎯⎯⎯⎯

(f) how to interview a person, obtain the desired information and reduce it to writing ⎯⎯⎯⎯

(g) how to recognize and preserve evidence ⎯⎯⎯⎯⎯⎯⎯⎯⎯⎯⎯⎯⎯⎯⎯⎯⎯

(h) how to use the Criminal Procedure Law, Penal Law and Vehicle & Traffic Law ⎯⎯⎯⎯

(i) about the Criminal Justice System ⎯⎯⎯⎯⎯⎯⎯⎯⎯⎯⎯⎯⎯⎯⎯⎯⎯⎯⎯⎯

(j) how to determine reasonable grounds for an arrest ⎯⎯⎯⎯⎯⎯⎯⎯⎯⎯⎯⎯⎯⎯

(k) how to develop criminal informants ⎯⎯⎯⎯⎯⎯⎯⎯⎯⎯⎯⎯⎯⎯⎯⎯⎯⎯⎯

(l) how to become a leader and assume responsibility ⎯⎯⎯⎯⎯⎯⎯⎯⎯⎯⎯⎯⎯⎯

(m) how much force to use in a given situation ⎯⎯⎯⎯⎯⎯⎯⎯⎯⎯⎯⎯⎯⎯⎯⎯

(n) how to identify the symptoms of drug abuse ⎯⎯⎯⎯⎯⎯⎯⎯⎯⎯⎯⎯⎯⎯⎯

(o) how to react correctly to a dangerous situation ⎯⎯⎯⎯⎯⎯⎯⎯⎯⎯⎯⎯⎯⎯⎯

(p) how to work on your own without supervision ⎯⎯⎯⎯⎯⎯⎯⎯⎯⎯⎯⎯⎯⎯⎯

(q) how to maintain your composure on the witness stand ⎯⎯⎯⎯⎯⎯⎯⎯⎯⎯⎯⎯

(r) how to recognize and deal with an agitator in a crowd ⎯⎯⎯⎯⎯⎯⎯⎯⎯⎯⎯⎯

(s) how to cross—examine a witness at a trial when acting as a prosecutor for your own arrests ⎯⎯

(t) how to shoot a revolver and shotgun accurately ⎯⎯⎯⎯⎯⎯⎯⎯⎯⎯⎯⎯⎯⎯

(u) proper circumstances under which you can take a human life ⎯⎯⎯⎯⎯⎯⎯⎯⎯⎯

(v) emergency removal of a child from a dangerous family situation ⎯⎯⎯⎯⎯⎯⎯⎯⎯

(w) distinctions between grades of crime ⎯⎯⎯⎯⎯⎯⎯⎯⎯⎯⎯⎯⎯⎯⎯⎯⎯⎯

(x) stop and frisk procedures ⎯⎯⎯⎯⎯⎯⎯⎯⎯⎯⎯⎯⎯⎯⎯⎯⎯⎯⎯⎯⎯⎯⎯

(y) regulations regarding reciprocity between states (for example, vehicles, weights and measures) ⎯⎯

SAMPLE ANNOUNCEMENT

TROOPER, NEW JERSEY STATE POLICE

The position of Trooper in the New Jersey State Police is open to any qualified person regardless of race, color, sex or religion.

Age: Between the ages of 18 and 35.

Driver's License: Must have a valid automobile driver's license.

Education: Must have a high school diploma or equivalent.

Vision: Vision must be not less than 20/30 in both eyes without glasses or contact lenses and absence of color blindness.

Written: Must pass a written examination. No prior application is necessary.

Medical: Must complete a medical questionnaire. Must pass a medical examination and have normal hearing in both ears.

Physical: Must pass a physical aptitude examination.

Investigation: Must have an excellent reputation. A thorough character investigation is made of each candidate.

Psychological: Candidates are given a psychological examination.

Oral Interview Board: Must successfully pass an Oral Interview Board.

Training: Candidates do not become sworn members until they have successfully completed an intensive pre-service training program.

Men and women who join the ranks of the State Police receive excellent salary, paid vacations, sick leave, free hospitalization, life insurance, uniforms and equipment. In addition, substantial retirement benefits are provided.

For further information write:

> **Recruiting and Research Unit**
> **New Jersey State Police**
> **Box 7068**
> **West Trenton, New Jersey 08625**

For information concerning civilian job opportunities with the New Jersey State Police contact:

> **Department of Civil Service**
> **East State and Montgomery Streets**
> **Trenton, New Jersey 08625**

THE KIND OF WORK YOU WILL BE DOING

This chapter provides essential information about the field in which you will be working. It gives you facts and figures concerning your chosen specialty and points up how desirable and interesting your job can be. When you know more about your job, you'll be more inclined to struggle and study for it.

NATURE OF THE WORK

The laws and regulations that govern the use of our nation's roadways are designed to insure the safety of all citizens. State troopers patrol our highways and enforce these laws.

State troopers issue traffic tickets to motorists who violate the law. At the scene of an accident, they direct traffic, give first aid, call for emergency equipment including ambulances, and write reports to be used in determining the cause of the accident.

In addition, state troopers provide services to motorists on the highways. For example, they radio for road service for drivers in mechanical trouble, direct tourists to their destination, or give information about lodging, restaurants, and tourist attractions.

State troopers also provide traffic assistance and control during road repairs, fires, and other emergencies, as well as for special occurrences such as parades and sports events. They sometimes check the weight of commercial vehicles, conduct driver examinations, and give information on highway safety to the public.

In addition to highway responsibilities, state troopers may investigate crimes, particularly in areas that do not have a police force. They sometimes help city or county police catch lawbreakers and control civil disturbances. State highway patrols, however, normally are restricted to vehicle and traffic matters.

Some troopers work with special state police units such as the mounted police, canine corps, and marine patrols. Others instruct trainees in state police schools, pilot police aircraft, or specialize in fingerprint classification or chemical and microscopic analysis of criminal evidence.

State troopers also write reports and maintain police records. Some troopers, including division or bureau chiefs responsible for training or investigation and those who command police operations in an assigned area, have administrative duties.

PLACES OF EMPLOYMENT

Many state troopers were employed last year. Although almost all were men, positions for women are expected to increase in the future.

The size of state forces varies considerably. The largest force (in California) has over 5,000 officers; the smallest (in North Dakota) has fewer than 100. One state (Hawaii) does not maintain a force.

TRAINING, OTHER QUALIFICATIONS, AND ADVANCEMENT

State civil service regulations govern the appointment of state troopers. All candidates must be citizens of the United States. Other entry requirements vary, but most states require that applicants have a high school education or an equivalent combination of education and experience and be at least 21 years old.

Troopers must pass a competitive examination and meet physical and personal qualifications. Physical requirements include standards of height, weight, and eyesight. Tests of strength and agility often are required. Because honesty and a sense of responsibility are important in police work, an applicant's character and background are investigated.

Although state troopers work independently, they must perform their duties in line with department rules. They should want to serve the public and be willing to work outdoors in all types of weather.

In all states, recruits enter a formal training program for several months. They receive classroom instruction in state laws and jurisdictions, and they study procedures for accident investigation, patrol, and traffic control. Recruits learn to use guns, defend themselves from attack, handle an automobile at high speeds, and give first aid. After gaining experience, some troopers take advanced training in police science, administration, law enforcement, or criminology. Classes are held at junior colleges, colleges and universities, or special police institutions such as the National Academy of the Federal Bureau of Investigation.

High school and college courses in English, government, psychology, sociology, American history, and physics help in preparing for a police career. Physical education and sports are useful for developing stamina and agility. Completion of a driver education course and training received in military police schools also are assets.

State trooper recruits serve a probationary period ranging from 6 months to 3 years. After a specified length of time, troopers become eligible for promotion. Most states have merit promotion systems that require troopers to pass a competitive examination to qualify for the next highest rank. Although the organization of police forces varies by state, the typical avenue of advancement is from private to corporal, to sergeant, to first sergeant, to lieutenant, and then to captain. State troopers who show administrative ability may be promoted to higher level jobs such as commissioner or director.

In some states, high school graduates may enter state police work as cadets. These paid civilian employees of the police organization attend classes to learn various aspects of police work and are assigned nonenforcement duties. Cadets who qualify may be appointed to the state police force at age 21.

EMPLOYMENT OUTLOOK

State trooper employment is expected to grow much faster than the average for other occupations. Although most jobs will result from this growth, some openings will be created as troopers retire, die or leave the occupation for other reasons. As job openings are filled from the ranks of available applicants, the increased interest of women in police work will result in greater employment of women for patrol duties.

Although some troopers will be needed in criminal investigation and other non-
way functions, the greatest demand will be for troopers to work in highway
ol. This is the result of a growing, more mobile population. In ever increas-
numbers, Americans are using the motor vehicle as a source of recreation.
rcycles, campers, and other recreational vehicles will continue to add to the
on's traffic flow and require additional officers to insure the safety of high-
users.
Because law enforcement work is becoming more complex, specialists will be need-
n crime laboratories and electronic data processing centers to develop admin-
ative and criminal information systems. However, in many departments, these
will be filled by civilian employees rather than uniformed officers.

NINGS AND WORKING CONDITIONS

Although starting salaries are normally higher in the West and lower in the
th, state troopers on the average earn about 1½ times as much as nonsupervi-
y workers in private industry, except farming.
State troopers generally receive regular increases, based on experience and
formance, until a specified maximum is reached.
State police agencies usually provide troopers with uniforms, firearms, and
er necessary equipment, or give special allowances for their purchase.
In many states, the scheduled workweek for state troopers is 40 hours. Although
workweek is longer in some states, hours over 40 are being reduced. Since
ice protection must be provided around the clock, some officers are on duty
r weekends, on holidays, and at night. State troopers also are subject to
rgency calls at any time.
State troopers usually are covered by liberal pension plans. Paid vacations,
k leave, and medical and life insurance plans frequently are provided.
The work of state troopers is sometimes dangerous. They always run the risk
an automobile accident while pursuing speeding motorists or fleeing criminals.
opers also face the risk of injury while apprehending criminals or controlling
orders.

RCES OF ADDITIONAL INFORMATION

Information about specific entrance requirements may be obtained from state
il service commissions or state police headquarters, usually located in each
te capital.

TECHNIQUES OF STUDY AND TEST-TAKING

Although a thorough knowledge of the subject matter is the most important factor in succeeding on your exam, the following suggestions could raise your score substantially. These few pointers will give you the strategy employed on tests by those who are most successful in this not-so-mysterious art. It's really quite simple. Do things right . . . right from the beginning. Make these successful methods a habit. Then you'll get the greatest dividends from the time you invest in this book.

PREPARING FOR THE EXAM

1. *Budget your time.* Set aside definite hours each day for concentrated study. Keep to your schedule.

2. *Study alone.* You will concentrate better when you work by yourself. Keep a list of questions you cannot answer and points you are unsure of to talk over with a friend who is preparing for the same exam. Plan to exchange ideas at a joint review session just before the test.

3. *Eliminate distractions.* Disturbances caused by family and neighbor activities (telephone calls, chit-chat, TV programs, etc.) work to your disadvantage. Study in a quiet, private room.

4. *Use the library.* Most colleges and universities have excellent library facilities. Some institutions have special libraries for the various subject areas: physics library, education library, psychology library, etc. Take full advantage of such valuable facilities. The library is free from those distractions that may inhibit your home study. Moreover, research in your subject area is more convenient in a library since it can provide more study material than you have at home.

5. *Answer all the questions in this book.* Don't be satisfied merely with the correct answer to each question. Do additional research on the other choices which are given. You will broaden your background and be more adequately prepared for the "real" exam. It's quite possible that a question on the exam which you are going to take may require you to be familiar with the other choices.

6. *Get the "feel" of the exam.* The sample questions which this book contains will give you that "feel" since they are virtually the same as those you will find on the test.

7. *Take the Sample Tests as "real" tests.* With this attitude, you will derive greater benefit. Put yourself under strict examination conditions. Tolerate no interruptions while you are taking the sample tests. Work steadily. Do not spend too much time on any one question. If a question seems too difficult go to the next one. If time permits, go back to the omitted question.

8. *Tailor your study to the subject matter. Skim or scan.* Don't study everything in the same manner. Obviously, certain areas are more important than others.

9. *Organize yourself.* Make sure that your notes are in good order—valuable time is unnecessarily consumed when you can't find quickly what you are looking for.

10. *Keep physically fit.* You cannot retain information well when you are uncomfortable, headachy, or tense. Physical health promotes mental efficiency.

HOW TO TAKE AN EXAM

1. *Get to the Examination Room about Ten Minutes Ahead of Time.* You'll get a better start when you are accustomed to the room. If the room is too cold, or too warm, or not well ventilated, call these conditions to the attention of the person in charge.

2. *Make Sure that You Read the Instructions Carefully.* In many cases, test-takers lose credits because they misread some important point in the given directions—example: the *incorrect* choice instead of the *correct* choice.

3. *Be Confident.* Statistics conclusively show that high scores are more likely when you are prepared. It is important to know that you are not expected to answer every question correctly. The questions usually have a range of difficulty and differentiate between several levels of skill.

4. *Skip Hard Questions and Go Back Later.* It is a good idea to make a mark on the question sheet next to all questions you cannot answer easily, and to go back to those questions later. First answer the questions you are sure about. Do not

panic if you cannot answer a question. Go on and answer the questions you know. Usually the easier questions are presented at the beginning of the exam and the questions become gradually more difficult.

If you do skip ahead on the exam, be sure to skip ahead also on your answer sheet. A good technique is periodically to check the number of the question on the answer sheet with the number of the question on the test. You should do this every time you decide to skip a question. If you fail to skip the corresponding answer blank for that question, all of your following answers will be wrong.

Each student is stronger in some areas than in others. No one is expected to know all the answers. Do not waste time agonizing over a difficult question because it may keep you from getting to other questions that you can answer correctly.

5. *Guess If You Are Not Sure*. No penalty is given for guessing when these exams are scored. Therefore, it is better to guess than to omit an answer.

6. *Mark the Answer Sheet Clearly*. When you take the examination, you will mark your answers to the multiple-choice questions on a separate answer sheet that will be given to you at the test center. If you have not worked with an answer sheet before, it is in your best interest to become familiar with the procedures involved. Remember, knowing the correct answer is not enough! If you do not mark the sheet correctly, so that it can be machine-scored, you will not get credit for your answers!

In addition to marking answers on the separate answer sheet, you will be asked to give your name and other information, including your social security number. As a precaution bring along your social security number for identification purposes.

Read the directions carefully and follow them exactly. If they ask you to print your name in the boxes provided, write only one letter in each box. If your name is longer than the number of boxes provided, omit the letters that do not fit. Remember, you are writing for a machine; it does not have judgment. It can only record the pencil marks you make on the answer sheet.

Use the answer sheet to record all your answers to questions. Each question, or item, has four or five answer choices labeled (A), (B), (C), (D), (E). You will be asked to choose the letter that stands for the best answer. Then you will be asked to mark your answer by blackening the appropriate space on your answer sheet. Be sure that each space you choose and blacken with your pencil is *completely* blackened. The machine will "read" your answers in terms of spaces blackened. Make sure that only one answer is clearly blackened. If you erase an answer, erase it completely and mark your new answer clearly. The machine will give credit only for clearly marked answers. It does not pause to decide whether you really meant (B) or (C).

Make sure that the number of the question you are being asked on the question sheet corresponds to the number of the question you are answering on the answer sheet. It is a good idea to check the numbers of questions and answers frequently. If you decide to skip a question, but fail to skip the corresponding answer blank for that question, all your answers after that will be wrong.

7. *Read Each Question Carefully*. The exam questions are not designed to trick you through misleading or ambiguous alternative choices. On the other hand, they are not all direct questions of factual information. Some are designed to elicit responses that reveal your ability to reason, or to interpret a fact or idea. It's up to you to read each question carefully, so you know what is being asked. The exam authors have tried to make the questions clear. Do not go astray looking for hidden meanings.

8. *Don't Answer Too Fast*. The multiple-choice questions which you will meet are not superficial exercises. They are designed to test not only your memory but also your understanding and insight. Do not place too much emphasis on speed. The time element is a factor, but it is not all-important. Accuracy should not be sacrificed for speed.

9. *Materials and Conduct at the Test Center*. You need to bring with you to the test center your Admission Form, your social security number, and several No. 2 pencils. Arrive on time as you may not be admitted after testing has begun. Instructions for taking the tests will be read to you by the test supervisor and time will be called when the test is over. If you have questions, you may ask them of the supervisor. Do not give or receive assistance while taking the exams. If you do, you will be asked to turn in all test materials and told to leave the room. You will not be permitted to return and your tests will not be scored.

2

PART TWO

First Sample Practice Examination

FIRST SAMPLE
PRACTICE EXAMINATION

Time allowed for the entire Examination: 3 Hours

In order to create the climate of the actual exam, that's exactly what you should allow yourself . . . no more, no less. Use a watch to keep a record of your time, since it might suit your convenience to try this practice exam in several short takes.

In constructing this Examination we tried to visualize the questions you are *likely* to face on your actual exam. We included those subjects on which they are *probably* going to test you.

Although copies of past exams are not released, we were able to piece together fairly complete pictures of some forthcoming exams.

A principal source of information was our analysis of official announcements going back several years.

Critical comparison of these announcements, particularly the sample questions, revealed the testing trend; foretold the important subjects, and those that are likely to recur.

The various subjects expected on the exams are represented by separate Tests.

The questions on each Test are represented exactly on the special Answer Sheet provided. Mark your answers on this sheet. It's just about the way you'll have to do it on the real exam.

Proceed through the entire exam without pausing after each Test. Remember that you are taking this Exam under actual battle conditions, and therefore you do not stop until told to do so by the proctor.

Certainly you should not lose time by trying to mark each Test as you complete it. You'll be able to score yourself fairly when time is up for the entire Exam.

Correct answers for all the questions in all the Tests of this Exam appear at the end of the Exam.

Don't cheat yourself by looking at these answers while taking the Exam. They are to be compared with your own answers *after* the time limit is up.

ANSWER SHEET FOR FIRST SAMPLE PRACTICE EXAMINATION

TEST I. JUDGMENT AND REASONING

1 Ⓐ Ⓑ Ⓒ Ⓓ	6 Ⓐ Ⓑ Ⓒ Ⓓ	11 Ⓐ Ⓑ Ⓒ Ⓓ	16 Ⓐ Ⓑ Ⓒ Ⓓ
2 Ⓐ Ⓑ Ⓒ Ⓓ	7 Ⓐ Ⓑ Ⓒ Ⓓ	12 Ⓐ Ⓑ Ⓒ Ⓓ	17 Ⓐ Ⓑ Ⓒ Ⓓ
3 Ⓐ Ⓑ Ⓒ Ⓓ	8 Ⓐ Ⓑ Ⓒ Ⓓ	13 Ⓐ Ⓑ Ⓒ Ⓓ	18 Ⓐ Ⓑ Ⓒ Ⓓ
4 Ⓐ Ⓑ Ⓒ Ⓓ	9 Ⓐ Ⓑ Ⓒ Ⓓ	14 Ⓐ Ⓑ Ⓒ Ⓓ	19 Ⓐ Ⓑ Ⓒ Ⓓ
5 Ⓐ Ⓑ Ⓒ Ⓓ	10 Ⓐ Ⓑ Ⓒ Ⓓ	15 Ⓐ Ⓑ Ⓒ Ⓓ	20 Ⓐ Ⓑ Ⓒ Ⓓ

TEST II. JUDGMENT AND REASONING

1 Ⓐ Ⓑ Ⓒ Ⓓ	4 Ⓐ Ⓑ Ⓒ Ⓓ	7 Ⓐ Ⓑ Ⓒ Ⓓ	10 Ⓐ Ⓑ Ⓒ Ⓓ	13 Ⓐ Ⓑ Ⓒ Ⓓ
2 Ⓐ Ⓑ Ⓒ Ⓓ	5 Ⓐ Ⓑ Ⓒ Ⓓ	8 Ⓐ Ⓑ Ⓒ Ⓓ	11 Ⓐ Ⓑ Ⓒ Ⓓ	14 Ⓐ Ⓑ Ⓒ Ⓓ
3 Ⓐ Ⓑ Ⓒ Ⓓ	6 Ⓐ Ⓑ Ⓒ Ⓓ	9 Ⓐ Ⓑ Ⓒ Ⓓ	12 Ⓐ Ⓑ Ⓒ Ⓓ	15 Ⓐ Ⓑ Ⓒ Ⓓ

TEST III. JUDGMENT AND REASONING

1 Ⓣ Ⓕ	7 Ⓣ Ⓕ	13 Ⓣ Ⓕ	19 Ⓣ Ⓕ	25 Ⓣ Ⓕ
2 Ⓣ Ⓕ	8 Ⓣ Ⓕ	14 Ⓣ Ⓕ	20 Ⓣ Ⓕ	26 Ⓣ Ⓕ
3 Ⓣ Ⓕ	9 Ⓣ Ⓕ	15 Ⓣ Ⓕ	21 Ⓣ Ⓕ	27 Ⓣ Ⓕ
4 Ⓣ Ⓕ	10 Ⓣ Ⓕ	16 Ⓣ Ⓕ	22 Ⓣ Ⓕ	28 Ⓣ Ⓕ
5 Ⓣ Ⓕ	11 Ⓣ Ⓕ	17 Ⓣ Ⓕ	23 Ⓣ Ⓕ	29 Ⓣ Ⓕ
6 Ⓣ Ⓕ	12 Ⓣ Ⓕ	18 Ⓣ Ⓕ	24 Ⓣ Ⓕ	30 Ⓣ Ⓕ

TEST IV. READING COMPREHENSION AND INTERPRETATION

1 Ⓐ Ⓑ Ⓒ Ⓓ	6 Ⓐ Ⓑ Ⓒ Ⓓ	11 Ⓐ Ⓑ Ⓒ Ⓓ	16 Ⓐ Ⓑ Ⓒ Ⓓ	21 Ⓐ Ⓑ Ⓒ Ⓓ
2 Ⓐ Ⓑ Ⓒ Ⓓ	7 Ⓐ Ⓑ Ⓒ Ⓓ	12 Ⓐ Ⓑ Ⓒ Ⓓ	17 Ⓐ Ⓑ Ⓒ Ⓓ	22 Ⓐ Ⓑ Ⓒ Ⓓ
3 Ⓐ Ⓑ Ⓒ Ⓓ	8 Ⓐ Ⓑ Ⓒ Ⓓ	13 Ⓐ Ⓑ Ⓒ Ⓓ	18 Ⓐ Ⓑ Ⓒ Ⓓ	23 Ⓐ Ⓑ Ⓒ Ⓓ
4 Ⓐ Ⓑ Ⓒ Ⓓ	9 Ⓐ Ⓑ Ⓒ Ⓓ	14 Ⓐ Ⓑ Ⓒ Ⓓ	19 Ⓐ Ⓑ Ⓒ Ⓓ	24 Ⓐ Ⓑ Ⓒ Ⓓ
5 Ⓐ Ⓑ Ⓒ Ⓓ	10 Ⓐ Ⓑ Ⓒ Ⓓ	15 Ⓐ Ⓑ Ⓒ Ⓓ	20 Ⓐ Ⓑ Ⓒ Ⓓ	25 Ⓐ Ⓑ Ⓒ Ⓓ

TEST V. READING COMPREHENSION AND INTERPRETATION

1 Ⓐ Ⓑ Ⓒ Ⓓ	6 Ⓐ Ⓑ Ⓒ Ⓓ	11 Ⓐ Ⓑ Ⓒ Ⓓ	16 Ⓐ Ⓑ Ⓒ Ⓓ
2 Ⓐ Ⓑ Ⓒ Ⓓ	7 Ⓐ Ⓑ Ⓒ Ⓓ	12 Ⓐ Ⓑ Ⓒ Ⓓ	17 Ⓐ Ⓑ Ⓒ Ⓓ
3 Ⓐ Ⓑ Ⓒ Ⓓ	8 Ⓐ Ⓑ Ⓒ Ⓓ	13 Ⓐ Ⓑ Ⓒ Ⓓ	18 Ⓐ Ⓑ Ⓒ Ⓓ
4 Ⓐ Ⓑ Ⓒ Ⓓ	9 Ⓐ Ⓑ Ⓒ Ⓓ	14 Ⓐ Ⓑ Ⓒ Ⓓ	19 Ⓐ Ⓑ Ⓒ Ⓓ
5 Ⓐ Ⓑ Ⓒ Ⓓ	10 Ⓐ Ⓑ Ⓒ Ⓓ	15 Ⓐ Ⓑ Ⓒ Ⓓ	

TEST VI. ARITHMETIC COMPUTATIONS

1 Ⓐ Ⓑ Ⓒ Ⓓ Ⓔ	4 Ⓐ Ⓑ Ⓒ Ⓓ Ⓔ	7 Ⓐ Ⓑ Ⓒ Ⓓ Ⓔ	10 Ⓐ Ⓑ Ⓒ Ⓓ Ⓔ	13 Ⓐ Ⓑ Ⓒ Ⓓ Ⓔ
2 Ⓐ Ⓑ Ⓒ Ⓓ Ⓔ	5 Ⓐ Ⓑ Ⓒ Ⓓ Ⓔ	8 Ⓐ Ⓑ Ⓒ Ⓓ Ⓔ	11 Ⓐ Ⓑ Ⓒ Ⓓ Ⓔ	14 Ⓐ Ⓑ Ⓒ Ⓓ Ⓔ
3 Ⓐ Ⓑ Ⓒ Ⓓ Ⓔ	6 Ⓐ Ⓑ Ⓒ Ⓓ Ⓔ	9 Ⓐ Ⓑ Ⓒ Ⓓ Ⓔ	12 Ⓐ Ⓑ Ⓒ Ⓓ Ⓔ	15 Ⓐ Ⓑ Ⓒ Ⓓ Ⓔ

TEST 1. JUDGMENT AND REASONING

DIRECTIONS: For each question read all the lettered choices carefully. Then select that answer which you consider correct or most nearly correct and complete. Blacken the lettered space on your answer sheet corresponding to your best selection, just as you would have to do on the actual examination.

The answer key appears at the end of all the tests in the examination.

1.   In addressing a class of recruits, an instructor remarked: "Carelessness and failure are twins." The one of the following that most nearly expresses the meaning of this statement is:
(A) negligence seldom accompanies success
(B) incomplete work is careless work
(C) conscientious work is never attended by failure
(D) a conscientious person never makes mistakes.

2.   In taking a statement from a person who has been shot by an assailant and is not expected to live, State Troopers are instructed to ask the person: "Do you believe you are about to die?" Of the following, the most probable reason for this question is:
(A) the theory that a person about to die and meet his Maker will tell the truth
(B) to determine if the victim is conscious and capable of making a statement
(C) to put the victim mentally at ease and more willing to talk
(D) that the statement could not be used in court if his mind was distraught by the fear of impending death.

3.   In lecturing on the law of arrest an instructor remarked: "To go beyond is as bad as to fall short." The one of the following which most nearly expresses the meaning of this statement is:
(A) never undertake the impossible
(B) extremes are not desirable
(C) look before you leap
(D) too much success is dangerous.

4.   As an intelligent State Trooper, you should know that, of the following, the one which is least likely to be followed by an increase in crime is:
(A) war   (B) depression
(C) poor housing (D) prosperity.

5.   As a State Trooper interested in the promotion of traffic safety, you should know that according to recent statistics, the one group which has the highest number of deaths as a result of being struck in traffic in large cities is:
(A) adults over 55 years of age
(B) adults between 36 and 55 years of age
(C) adults between 22 and 35 years old
(D) children up to 4 years old.

6.   As an intelligent State Trooper having a knowledge of the various types of crime, you should know that in recent years, the age group 16 through 25 showed the greatest number of arrests in New York City for:
(A) grand larceny from highways and vehicles
(B) burglary
(C) rape
(D) homicide.

7.   As a State Trooper interested in the reduction of unnecessary traffic accidents, you should know that two of the chief sources of such accidents to pedestrians in recent years were:

(A) crossing a street against the light, and crossing past a parked car
(B) crossing a street at a point other than the crossing, and crossing against the light
(C) crossing a street at a point other than the crossing, and running off the sidewalk
(D) crossing a street against the light, and failing to observe whether cars were making right or left turns.

8.　　　A "modus operandi" file will be most valuable to a new State Trooper as a means of showing the:
(A) methods used by criminals
(B) various bureaus and divisions of the Police Department
(C) number and nature of vehicular accidents
(D) forms used by the Police Department.

9.　　　A State Trooper is frequently advised to lie down before returning fire, if a person is shooting at him or her. This is primarily because:
(A) a smaller target will thus be presented to the assailant
(B) he or she can return fire more quickly while in the prone position
(C) the assailant will think the trooper has been struck and cease firing
(D) it will indicate that the trooper is not the aggressor

10.　　　In making arrests during a large riot, it is the practice for troopers to take the ringleaders into custody as soon as possible. This is primarily because:
(A) the police can obtain valuable information from them
(B) They deserve punishment more than the other rioters
(C) rioters need leadership and, without it, will disperse more quickly
(D) arrests of wrongdoers should always be in order of their importance.

11.　　　As you are patrolling your post, you observe two men running toward a parked automobile in which a driver is seated. You question the three men and you note the license number. You should:
(A) let them go if you see nothing suspicious
(B) warn them not to be caught loitering again
(C) arrest them because they have probably committed a crime
(D) take them back with you to the place from which the two men came.

12.　　　Assume that you are a State Trooper. A woman has complained to you about a man's indecent exposure in front of a house. As you approach the house, the man begins to run. You should:
(A) shoot to kill as the man may be a dangerous maniac
(B) fire a warning shot to try to halt the man
(C) summon other troopers in order to apprehend him
(D) question the woman regarding the man's identity.

13.　　　You are patrolling a parkway in a radio car with another Trooper. A maroon car coming from the opposite direction signals you to stop and the driver informs you that he was robbed by three men speeding ahead of him in a black sedan. Your radio car cannot cross the center abutment. You should:
(A) request the driver to make a report to the nearest precinct as your car cannot cross over to the other side
(B) make a U turn in your radio car and give chase on the wrong side of the parkway
(C) fire warning shots in the air to summon other Troopers
(D) flash headquarters over your radio system.

14. You notice that a man is limping hurriedly, leaving a trail of blood behind him. You question him and his explanation is that he was hurt accidentally while he was watching a man clean a gun. You should:
(A) let him go as you have no proof that his story is not true
(B) take him to the nearest city hospital and question him again after treatment
(C) ask him whether the man had a license for his gun
(D) ask him to lead you to the man who cleaned his gun so that you may question him further about the accident.

15. Which of the following situations, if observed by you while on patrol, should you consider most suspicious and deserving of further investigation?
(A) A shabbily dressed youth is driving a late model Buick.
(B) A 1968 Dodge has been parked without lights outside an apartment house for several hours.
(C) A light is on in the rear of a one-family luxurious residence.
(D) Two well-dressed men are standing at a bus stop at 2 A.M. and arguing heatedly.

16. In addition to cases of submersion, artificial respiration is a recommended first aid procedure for:
(A) sunstroke
(B) chemical poisoning
(C) electrical shock
(D) apoplexy.

17. An injury to a muscle or tendon brought about by severe exertion and resulting in pain and stiffness is called a:
(A) strain   (B) sprain
(C) bruise   (D) fracture.

18. The delivery of an arrested person to his sureties, upon their giving security for his appearance at the time and place designated to submit to the jurisdiction and judgment of the court, is known as:
(A) bail   (B) habeas corpus
(C) parole   (D) probation.

19. Jones was charged with the murder of Smith. Brown, Jones' landlord testified at the trial that Jones had in his home a well-equipped laboratory which contained all the necessary chemicals for producing the poison which an autopsy showed caused Smith's death. Brown's testimony constitutes what is called:
(A) corroborative evidence
(B) opinion evidence
(C) hearsay evidence
(D) circumstantial evidence.

20. The procedure, whereby a defendant is brought before a magistrate, is informed of the charge against him and is asked how he pleads thereto, is called:
(A) arraignment   (B) indictment
(C) presentment   (D) inquisition.

END OF TEST

Go on to the next test in the examination, just as you would do on the actual exam. Check your answers when you have completed the entire examination. The answer key for this test, and all the other tests, will be found at the conclusion of the examination.

TEST II. JUDGMENT AND REASONING

DIRECTIONS: For each question read all the choices carefully. Then select that answer which you consider correct or most nearly correct. Blacken the answer space corresponding to your best choice, just as you would do on the actual examination.

1. It is customary for state police to keep records of lost or stolen automobile license plates. Of the following, the best reason for this practice is to
   (A) permit the prompt issuance of new plates
   (B) keep a record of all outstanding license plates in use
   (C) prevent cars from being stolen
   (D) capture or detain any person found using or attempting to use any of these plates.

2. A "modus operandi" file will be most valuable to a new State Trooper as a means of showing the
   (A) methods used by criminals
   (B) various bureaus and divisions of the Police Department
   (C) number and nature of vehicular accidents
   (D) forms used by the Police Department.

3. One of the chief reasons why fingerprints are of great value in helping to identify people is that
   (A) criminals always leave fingerprints at the scene of a crime, whether they know it or not
   (B) no two persons have the same fingerprint pattern
   (C) fingerprint patterns change as people grow older
   (D) nationality, religion and race can be determined by fingerprint patterns.

4. It is least accurate to state of fingerprints that
   (A) it is possible to fingerprint even a dead person
   (B) the value of fingerprints left at the scene of a crime does not vary with the distinctness of the fingerprint impressions
   (C) no fingerprints of different persons have ever been found to be alike
   (D) the prime value of fingerprints lies in their effectiveness in identifying people.

5. Of the following, the one which is *least* a purpose of fingerprinting procedure is the
   (A) identification of deceased persons.
   (B) identification of the guilty
   (C) protection of the innocent
   (D) recognition of first offenders.

6. It is suggested that a suspect should not be permitted to walk in or about the scene of a crime where fingerprints may be present until a thorough search has been made for such evidence. This suggested procedure is
   (A) good; the suspect would, if permitted to walk about the scene, smear all fingerprints that might be found by police investigators
   (B) bad; the return of a suspect to the scene of a crime provides an opportunity to obtain additional fingerprints from the suspect
   (C) good; if the suspect handled any objects at the scene, the value of any original fingerprints, as evidence, might be seriously impaired

(D) bad; the return of a suspect to the scene of a crime provides an opportunity to identify objects that had been handled during the commission of the crime.

7. According to the Manual of Procedure, the delivery, for laboratory examination, of any article required as evidence must be made by the member of the force finding or coming into the possession of such evidence. Of the following, the most likely reason for this procedure is that it
(A) assists in the establishment of the authenticity of the evidence
(B) encourages a more careful search of the crime scene for all physical evidence that may be related to the crime
(C) insures that the evidence will be properly marked or tagged for future identification
(D) prevents the undue delay which might result from a delivery through official channels.

8. A certain trooper brought a bullet to a scientific crime laboratory for examination. The officer produced the bullet from his pocket and with it money and a penknife which were his personal property. The officer had carried the bullet for several days in his pocket in this manner. His action in this case is
(A) not proper, since the value of ballistics analysis of the bullet has probably been largely decreased
(B) intelligent, since his technique of preserving the bullet practically eliminates the possibility of losing the bullet
(C) intelligent, since no harm has been done and the entire matter has been handled without the undue expenditure of time or effort
(D) not proper, because evidence of this type necessarily decreases in value if carried on one's person for more than a maximum of 24 hours.

9. Of the following, the most accurate characterization of the value of the scientific laboratory to a police force is that the laboratory is
(A) a supplement to the work of the police officer
(B) destined eventually to replace the police officer

(C) a device, especially useful in detective work, without which police officers could hope to solve only a small percentage of crimes committed
(D) useful as an instrument for the prevention of crime but likely to be grossly fallible as a device to help solve crimes actually committed.

10. 'Moulage" is
(A) a system of personal identification
(B) a plastic material used for making casts of objects
(C) a narcotic drug
(D) criminal parlance for "money."

11. The use of truth serum (scopolamine)
(A) is authorized by the Code of Criminal Procedure
(B) is specifically outlawed by the Penal Law
(C) is regarded as a violation of the privilege against self-incrimination
(D) needs no statutory sanction.

12. Poroscopy is
(A) the science of identification through the sweat pores
(B) the science of microscopic hair analysis
(C) a term applied to art or literature of an obscene nature
(D) the science of determining the mineral content of soil.

13. The method of lie detection which has the greatest possibility of danger to the life of the suspect is
(A) the polygraph
(B) Pneumograph
(C) Psychogalvanometer
(D) scopolamine.

14. Suppose you are checking an alphabetical card reference file to locate information about a "George Dyerly." After checking all the "D's" you can find a card only for a "George Dyrely." Of the following the best action for you to take is to

(A) check the balance of the file to see if the card you are interested in has been misfiled
(B) check the data on the card to see if it relates to the same person in whom you are interested
(C) correct the spelling of the name on your records and reports to conform to the spelling on the card
(D) reject this reference file as a source of information regarding this person.

15. "The Bertillon system, which is based on physical measurements, is in some respects superior to fingerprints as a method of identification." Of the following, the best justification for this statement is that such measurements

(A) cannot be altered by the criminal
(B) are more individually characteristic than fingerprints
(C) are easier to take than fingerprints
(D) can be made as precise as desirable.

END OF TEST

Go on to the next test in the examination, just as you would do on the actual exam. Check your answers when you have completed the entire examination. The answer key for this test, and all the other tests, will be found at the conclusion of the examination.

TEST III. JUDGMENT AND REASONING

DIRECTIONS: Each of the following statements is either True or False. Mark the corresponding number on your answer sheet T if the statement is True, and F if the statement is False.

1. In an emergency it is best for a State Trooper to use personal judgment rather than follow the dictates of superior officers.

2. **The testimony of an eye witness is always reliable.**

3. **Every traffic violator is a unique individual and must be handled differently from others.**

4. **If you feel that a superior officer is treating you unfairly, it is best to express your feeling by refusing complete cooperation at intervals.**

5. A State Trooper on night duty should vary the route and schedule of patrol.

6. **The infliction of the death penalty for a crime is often referred to as corporal punishment.**

7. The prime requisites of the efficient State Trooper are a good physique and a commanding appearance.

8. **A felony is a more serious crime than a misdemeanor.**

9. The term recidivist has to do with psychiatric treatment.

10. **If you notice a fellow Trooper struggling violently with a prisoner, the first thing you should do is run for assistance.**

11. **Reading, writing, and holding conversation, while on duty should properly be limited to that necessary in the discharge of duty, whether it be with violators of the law or fellow Troopers.**

12. Never bully a motorist guilty of speeding unless he or she seems impressed by your attitude.

13. **A crime may be punishable only by death or imprisonment.**

14. Never call for additional assistance if you feel you can handle an unruly or violent criminal yourself.

15. If your supervising officer were to criticize you severely in the presence of fellow Troopers, it would be best to make no reply and thereafter refuse to speak to that officer.

16. A Trooper who wilfully permits a prisoner's escape is guilty of a felony.

17. An accomplice is one who has had some part in the commission of a crime.

18. The term habeas corpus refers to a writ directing that a detained or imprisoned person be brought into court regarding the lawfulness of his or her detention.

19. A trooper may not search a motorist's car, in the line of duty, without first having received orders from an immediate superior.

20. A State Trooper should remain on duty until properly relieved, even if the relief Trooper is two hours late in reporting.

21. The indeterminate sentence is like the suspended sentence in that the offender is not placed in prison after conviction.

22. It is proper for a State Trooper to exchange posts with another Trooper without the permission of the supervising officer, if the exchange in no way affects discipline or routine.

23. The right of persons against unreasonable searches and seizures is provided for in the United States Constitution.

24. No two fingerprints are exactly alike.

25. The quality most desired in a State Trooper is ability to shoot straight.

26. A State Trooper should enforce all the rules of the department even though he or she believes them to be unjust.

27. The protection of society is a minor function of a State Trooper.

28. The state seeking a fugitive from justice is known as the demanding state.

29. Emotional instability is a common causal factor in the commission of crime.

30. The crime of mayhem has to do with the willful and malicious delay of payment of a debt.

END OF TEST

TEST IV. READING COMPREHENSION AND INTERPRETATION

DIRECTIONS: This test consists of several reading passages, each followed by a number of statements. Analyze each statement solely on the basis of the material given. Then, mark your answer sheet (A) (B) (C) or (D).
Mark it (A) if the statement is entirely true.
Mark it (B) if the statement is entirely false.
Mark it (C) if the statement is partially false and partially true.
Mark it (D) if the statement cannot be judged on the basis of the facts given in the excerpt.

READING PASSAGE

"A prisoner, who, being confined in a prison, or being in lawful custody of an officer or other person, escapes from such prison or custody, is guilty of a felony if such custody or confinement is upon a charge, arrest, commitment, or conviction for a felony, and of a misdemeanor if such custody or confinement is upon a charge, arrest, commitment or conviction for a misdemeanor. A prisoner confined in a state prison for a term less than for life, who attempts, although unsuccessfully, to escape from such prison, is guilty of felony."

1. An unsuccessful attempt at escape from a state prison is not generally punishable.

2. A recaptured state convict serving less than a life sentence, is reimprisoned for life upon recapture.

3. A prisoner, having been arrested on a misdemeanor charge is guilty of a felony if he makes a successful attempt at escape but is later recaptured.

4. A person charged with a misdemeanor, being held in legal custody, is guilty of a misdemeanor in the event of an escape from custody and later recapture.

5. A prisoner, not under a life sentence, confined to a state prison, is deemed guilty of a felony if he or she makes a successful attempt at escape, and is subsequently recaptured, but if the attempt is unsuccessful, the prisoner is guilty of a misdemeanor.

READING PASSAGE

"A person, who, with intent to effect or facilitate the escape of a prisoner, whether the escape is effected or attempted or not, enters a prison, or conveys to a prisoner any information, or sends into a prison any disguise, instrument, weapon, or other thing, is guilty of felony, if the prisoner is held upon a charge, arrest, commitment, or conviction for a felony; and of a misdemeanor, if the prisoner is held upon a charge, arrest, commitment, or conviction of a misdemeanor."

6. A person sending a misdemeanant a weapon with intent to effect that person's getting away is liable to arrest under the charge of felony.

7. Entering a state prison for the sole purpose of conveying information to a prisoner is not legally punishable.

8. The intent to effect the escape of a state prisoner, is not punished as severely as an actual attempt.

9. Any attempt on the part of an outside person to facilitate the escape of a felon is punishable as a felony.

10. The act of conveying to a prisoner of a disguise is in itself punishable as either a misdemeanor or a felony.

READING PASSAGE

"A sheriff, or other officer or person, who allows a prisoner, lawfully in his custody, in any action or proceedings, civil or criminal, or in any prison under his charge or control, to escape or go at large, except as permitted by law, or connives at or assists such escape, or omits an act or duty whereby such escape is occasioned, or contributed to, or assisted is: 1. If he corruptly and wilfully allows, connives at, or assists the escape, guilty of a felony; 2. In any other case, is guilty of a misdemeanor. Any officer who is convicted of the offense specified, forfeits his office, and is forever disqualified to hold any office, or place of trust, honor, or profit, under the constitution or laws of this state."

11. If a prisoner escapes from a guard through no fault of the latter, the guard is not liable to any action.

12. A prison guard assisting the escape of a felon, is himself open to a charge constituting felony.

13. A person having legal custody over a prisoner, and who unlawfully permits his freedom, is liable to forfeiture of his office if action against the prisoner is criminal, but is not so liable if civil.

14. A guard who through negligence in his duty permits a prisoner to escape, is not open to a criminal charge.

15. A sheriff illegally permitting a prisoner in a civil action, not under a charge of felony, to go at large, may be punished as a misdemeanant.

READING PASSAGE

"A person who gives or offers a bribe to any executive officer, or to a person elected or appointed to become an executive officer, of this state with intent to influence that person in respect to any act, decision, vote, opinion, or other proceedings as such officer, is punishable by imprisonment in a state prison not exceeding ten years or by a fine not exceeding five thousand dollars, or by both."

16. An elected executive officer may not generally be punished for accepting a small bribe.

17. An appointed executive officer convicted of accepting a bribe may be punished by either fine or imprisonment.

18. Bribing of an executive officer with intent to influence the officer's vote, is deemed a criminal act, and in certain instances may be punishable by life imprisonment.

19. The length of a sentence to which a person is liable upon conviction for offering a bribe to an executive officer is limited to ten years.

20. An executive officer accepting a bribe is equally guilty with the person offering the bribe, though the punishment is not as severe.

READING PASSAGE

"A Commissioner of Correction, warden or other officer or prison guard, employed at any of the prisons who: 1. Shall be directly or indirectly interested in any contract, purchase of sale, for, by, or on account of such prison; or, 2. Accepts a present from a contractor or contractor's agent, directly or indirectly, or employs the labor of a convict or another person employed in such prison on any work for the private benefit of such commissioner, warden or guard, is guilty of a misdemeanor, except that the warden shall be entitled to employ prisoners for necessary household service."

21. A guard who employs the labor of prisoners in his or her own interests is guilty of a misdemeanor, except that such labor may be so employed indirectly.

22. Only a Commissioner of Correction may accept a small present from a contractor, and then only indirectly.

23. In no case may a prison guard be directly interested in a contract in which the prison is a party.

24. It is illegal to employ the labor of a convict in any case.

25. A warden may only indirectly be interested in the sale of merchandise on account of the prison at which he or she is employed.

TEST V. READING COMPREHENSION AND INTERPRETATION

This test of your ability to comprehend what you read consists of a number of different passages. One or more questions are based on each passage. Questions consist of incomplete statements about a passage. Each incomplete statement is followed by four choices lettered (A), (B), (C) and (D). Mark your answer sheet with the letter of that choice which best conveys the meaning of the passage, and which best completes the statement.

The answer key for this test will be found at the end of the examination.

Questions 1 through 8 are based on the following excerpt from an Annual Report of a Police Department. This material should be read first and then referred to in answering these questions, which are to be answered solely on the basis of the material herein contained.

LEGAL BUREAU

"One of the more important functions of this bureau is to analyze and furnish the department with pertinent information concerning Federal and State statues and Local Laws which affect the department, law enforcement or crime prevention. In addition, all measures introduced in the State Legislature and the City Council, which may affect this department are carefully reviewed by members of the Legal Bureau and where necessary, opinions and recommendations thereon are prepared

"Another important function of this office is the prosecution of cases in the Magistrate's Courts This is accomplished by assignment of attorneys who are members of the Legal Bureau to appear in those cases which are deemed to raise issues of importance to the department or questions of law which require technical presentation to facilitate proper determination; and also in those cases where request is made for such appearances by a magistrate, some other official of the city, or a member of the force. Attorneys are regularly assigned to prosecute all cases in the Women's Court.

"Proposed legislation was prepared and sponsored for introduction in the State Legislature and, at this writing, one of these proposals has already been enacted into law and five others are presently on the Governor's desk awaiting executive action. The new law prohibits the sale or possession of a hypodermic syringe or needle by an unauthorized person. The bureau's proposals awaiting executive action pertain to: an amendment to the Code of Criminal Procedure prohibiting desk officers from taking bail in gambling cases or in cases mentioned in Section 552, Code of Criminal Procedure; including confidence men and swindlers as jostlers in the Penal Law; prohibiting the sale of switch-blade knives of any size of children under 16 and bills extending the licensing period of gunsmiths.

"The following is a statistical report of the activities of the bureau during Year 2 as compared with Year 1:

	Year 2	Year 1
Memoranda of law prepared	83	68
Legal matters forwarded to Corporation Counsel	122	144
Letters requesting legal information	756	807
Letters requesting departmental records	139	111
Matters for publication	26	17
Court appearances of members of bureau	4,678	4,621
Conferences	94	103
Lectures at Police Academy	30	33
Reports on proposed legislation	255	194
Deciphering of codes	79	27
Expert testimony	31	16
Notices to court witnesses	81	55
Briefs prepared	22	18
Court papers prepared	258	260

1.   One of the functions of the Legal Bureau is to:
(A) review and make recommendations on proposed Federal laws affecting law enforcement
(B) prepare opinions on all measures introduced in the State legislature and the City Council
(C) furnish the Department with pertinent information concerning all new Federal and State laws
(D) analyze all laws affecting the work of the Department.

2.   The one of the following that is not a function of the Legal Bureau is:
(A) law enforcement and crime prevention
(B) prosecution of all cases in Women's Court
(C) prosecute cases in Magistrate's Court
(D) lecturing at the Police Academy.

3.   Members of the Legal Bureau frequently appear in Magistrate's Court for the purpose of:
(A) defending members of the Department
(B) raising issues of importance to the Department
(C) prosecuting all offenders arrested by the members of the Department
(D) facilitating proper determination of questions of law requiring technical presentaiton.

4.   The Legal Bureau sponsored a bill that would:
(A) extend the licenses of gunsmiths

(B) prohibit the sale of switchblade knives to children of any size
(C) place confidence men and swindlers in the same category as jostlers in the Penal Law
(D) prohibit desk officers from admitting gamblers, confidence men and swindlers to bail.

5.   From the report it is not reasonable to infer that:
(A) fewer bills affecting the Department were introduced in Year 2
(B) the preparation of court papers was a new activity assumed in Year 2
(C) the Code of Criminal Procedure authorizes desk officers to accept bail in certain cases
(D) the penalty for jostling and swindling is the same.

6.   According to the statistical report, the activity showing the greatest percentage of increase in Year 2 as compared with Year 1 was:
(A) matters of publication
(B) reports on proposed legislation
(C) notices to court witnesses
(D) memoranda of law prepared.

7.   According to the statistical report, the activity showing the greatest percentage of increase in Year 2 as compared with Year 1 was:
(A) court appearances of members of the Bureau
(B) giving expert testimony
(C) deciphering of codes
(D) letters requesting departmental records.

8. According to the report, the percentage of bills prepared and sponsored by the Legal Bureau which were passed by the State Legislature and sent to the Governor for approval was:
(A) approximately 3.1%
(B) approximately 2.6%
(C) approximately .5%
(D) not capable of determination from the data given.

Answer questions 9 to 12 on the basis of the following statement:
Disorderly conduct, in the abstract, does not constitute any crime known to law; it is only when it tends to a breach of the peace under the circumstances detailed in section 1458 of the Consolidation Act, that it constitutes a minor offense cognizable by the judge and when it in fact threatens to disturb the peace it is a misdemeanor as well as under section 675 of the Penal Code as at common law, and not within the jurisdiction of the judge, but of the Criminal Court.

9. Of the following, the most accurate statement on the basis of the preceding paragraph is that:
(A) an act which merely threatens to disturb the peace is not a crime
(B) disorderly conduct, by itself, is not a crime
(C) some types of disorderly conduct are indictable
(D) a minor offense may or may not be cognizable.

10. Of the following, the least accurate statement of the basis of the preceding paragraph is that:
(A) disorderly conduct which threatens to disturb the peace is within the jurisdiction of the judge
(B) disorderly conduct which "tends to a breach of the peace" may constitute a minor offense
(C) Section 1458 of the Consolidation Act discusses a "breach of the peace"
(D) disorderly conduct which "tends to a breach of the peace" is not the same as that which threatens to disturb the peace.

11. The preceding paragraph distinguishes least sharply between:

(A) jurisdiction of a judge and jurisdiction of the Criminal Court
(B) disorderly conduct as a crime and disorderly conduct as no crime
(C) what "tends to a breach of the peace" and what threatens to disturb the peace
(D) a minor offense and a misdemeanor.

12. Of the following generalizations, the one which is best illustrated by the preceding paragraph is that:
(A) acts which in themselves are not criminal may become criminal as a result of their effect
(B) abstract conduct may, in and of itself, be criminal
(C) criminal acts are determined by results rather than by intent
(D) an act which is criminal to begin with may not be criminal if it fails to have the desired effect.

Questions 13 and 14 pertain to the following section of the Penal Code:
"Section 1942. A person who, after having been three times convicted within this state, of felonies or attempts to commit felonies, or under the law of any other state, government or country, of crimes which if committed within this state would become felonious, commits a felony, other than murder, first or second degree, or treason, within this state, shall be sentenced upon conviction of such fourth, or subsequent, offense to imprisonment in a state prison for an indeterminate term the maximum of which shall not be less than the maximum term provided for first offenders for the crime for which the individual has been convicted, but, in any event, the minimum term upon conviction for a felony as the fourth or subsequent offense, shall not be less than fifteen years, and the maximum thereof shall be his natural life."

13. Under the terms of the quoted portion of Section 1942 of the Penal Law, a person must receive the increased punishment therein provided if:
(A) he is convicted of a felony and has been three times previously convicted of felonies
(B) he has been three times previously convicted of felonies, regardless of the nature of his present conviction
(C) his fourth conviction is for murder, first or second degree, or treason

(D) he has previously been convicted three times of murder, first or second degree, or treason.

14.　　　Under the terms of the quoted portion of Section 1942 of the Penal Law, a person convicted of a felony for which the penalty is imprisonment for a term not to exceed ten years, and who has been three times previously convicted of felonies in this state, shall be sentenced to a term the minimum of which shall be:
(A) ten years
(B) fifteen years
(C) indeterminate
(D) his natural life.

　　　In answering questions 15 to 19 the following definitions of crimes should be applied, bearing in mind that all elements contained in the definition must be present in order to charge a person with that crime:

　　　BURGLARY is the breaking and entering a building with intent to commit some crime therein.

　　　EXTORTION is the obtaining of property from another, with his consent, induced by a wrongful use of force or fear, or under color of official right.

　　　LARCENY is the taking and carrying away of the personal property of another with intent to deprive or defraud the owner of the use and benefit of such property.

　　　ROBBERY is the unlawful taking of the personal property of another from his person or in his presence, by force or violence or by putting him in fear of injury, immediate or future, to his person or property.

15.　　　If A entered B's store during business hours, tied B to a chair and then helped himself to the contents of B's cash register, A upon arrest, should be charged with:
(A) burglary　　(B) extortion
(C) larceny　　(D) robbery.

16.　　　If A broke the panel of glass in the window of B's store stepped in and removed some merchandise from the window, he should, upon arrest, be charged with:
(A) burglary　　(B) extortion
(C) larceny　　(D) robbery.

17.　　　If A, after B had left for the day, found the door of B's store open, walked in, took some merchandise and then left through the same door, he should, upon arrest, be charged with:
(A) burglary　　(B) extortion
(C) larceny　　(D) robbery.

18.　　　If A, by threatening to report B for failure to pay to the City the full amount of sales tax he had collected from various customers, induced B to give him the contents of his cash register, A should, upon arrest, be charged with:
(A) burglary　　(B) extortion
(C) larceny　　(D) robbery.

19.　　　If A, on a crowded train, put his hand into B's pocket and removed B's wallet without his knowledge, A should, upon arrest, be charged with:
(A) burglary　　(B) extortion
(C) larceny　　(D) robbery.

END OF TEST

Go on to do the following Test in this Examination, just as you would be expected to do on the actual exam.

TEST VI. ARITHMETIC COMPUTATIONS

TIME: 15 Minutes. 15 Questions.

DIRECTIONS: Each problem in this test involves a certain amount of logical reasoning and thinking on your part, besides the usual simple computations, to help you in finding the solution. Read each problem carefully and choose the correct answer from the five choices that follow. Mark E as your answer if none of the suggested answers agree with your answer. When you have finished, check your answers with the answer key at the end of the examination.

1. Find the interest on $25,800 for 144 days at 6% per annum. Base your calculations on a 360-day year.

   (A) $619.20   (B) $619.02
   (C) $691.02   (D) $691.20
           (E) None of these

2. A court clerk estimates that the untried cases on the docket will occupy the court for 150 trial days. If new cases are accumulating at the rate of 1.6 trial days per day (Saturday and Sunday excluded) and the court sits 5 days a week, how many days' business will remain to be heard at the end of 60 trial days?

   (A) 168 trial days   (B) 185 trial days
   (C) 188 trial days   (D) 186 trial days
           (E) None of these

3. The visitors section of a courtroom seats 105 people. The court is in session 6 hours of the day. On one particular day 486 people visited the court and were given seats. What is the average length of time spent by each visitor in the court? Assume that as soon as a person leaves a seat it is immediately filled and that at no time during the day is one of the 105 seats vacant. Express your answer in hours and minutes.

   (A) 1 hr. 20 min.   (B) 1 hr. 18 min.
   (C) 1 hr. 30 min.   (D) 2 hr.
           (E) None of these

4.
   If paper costs $2.92 per ream and 5% discount is allowed for cash, how many reams can be purchased for $138.70 cash? Do not discard fractional part of a cent in your calculations.

   (A) 49 reams   (B) 60 reams
   (C) 50 reams   (D) 53 reams
           (E) None of these

5. How much time is there between 8:30 a.m. today and 3:15 a.m. tomorrow.

   (A) 17¾ hrs.   (B) 18 hrs.
   (C) 18⅔ hrs.   (D) 18½ hrs.
           (E) None of these

6. How many days are there between September 19th and December 25th, both inclusive?

   (A) 98 days   (B) 96 days
   (C) 89 days   (D) 90 days
           (E) None of these

7. A clerk is requested to file 800 cards. If the clerk can file cards at a rate of 80 cards an hour, the number of cards remaining to be filed after 7 hours work is

   (A) 40   (B) 250
   (C) 140   (D) 260
           (E) None of these

8. An officer's weekly expenses are increased from $400.00 to $450.00. The percent of increase is, most nearly

   (A) 10 per cent   (B) 11 1/9 per cent
   (C) 12½ per cent   (D) 14 1/7 per cent
           (E) None of these

9. If there are 245 sections in the city, the average number of sections for each of the 5 boroughs is

(A) 50 sections   (B) 49 sections
(C) 47 sections   (D) 59 sections
      (E) None of these

10. If a section had 45 miles of street to plow after a snow storm and 9 plows are used, each plow would cover an average of how many miles?

    (A) 7 miles   (B) 6 miles
    (C) 8 miles   (D) 5 miles
      (E) None of these

11. If a crosswalk plow engine is run 5 minutes a day for ten days in a given month, it would run how long in the course of this month?

    (A) 50 min.   (B) 1½ hrs.
    (C) 1 hr.   (D) 30 min.
      (E) None of these

12. If the department uses 1500 workers in manual street cleaning and half as many more to load and drive trucks, the total number used is

    (A) 2200 workers   (B) 2520 workers

(C) 2050 workers   (D) 2250 workers
      (E) None of these

13. If an inspector issued 186 summonses in the course of 7 hours, his hourly average of summonses issued was

    (A) 23 summonses   (B) 26 summonses
    (C) 25 summonses   (D) 28 summonses
      (E) None of these

14. If, of 186 summonses issued, one hundred were issued to first offenders, then there were how many summonses issued to other than first offenders?

    (A) 68   (B) 90
    (C) 86   (D) 108
      (E) None of these

15. A truck going at a rate of 20 miles an hour will reach a town 40 miles away in how many hours?

    (A) 3 hrs.   (B) 1 hr.
    (C) 4 hrs.   (D) 5 hrs.
      (E) None of these

END OF EXAMINATION

If you finish before the allotted time is up, check your work. When time runs out, compare your answers for this test and all the other tests in the examination with the answer key that follows.

ANSWER KEY FOR FIRST SAMPLE PRACTICE EXAMINATION

TEST I. JUDGMENT AND REASONING

1.A	4.D	7.B	10.A	13.D	16.C	19.D
2.A	5.A	8.A	11.A	14.B	17.A	20.A
3.B	6.B	9.A	12.B	15.A	18.A	

TEST II. JUDGMENT AND REASONING

1.D	4.B	7.A	10.B	13.D
2.A	5.D	8.A	11.D	14.B
3.B	6.C	9.C	12.A	15.A

TEST III. JUDGMENT AND REASONING

1.F	5.T	9.F	13.F	17.T	21.F	25.F	28.T
2.F	6.T	10.F	14.F	18.T	22.F	26.T	29.T
3.T	7.F	11.T	15.F	19.F	23.T	27.F	30.F
4.F	8.T	12.F	16.T	20.T	24.T		

TEST IV. READING COMPREHENSION AND INTERPRETATION

1.B	5.C	8.B	11.D	14.B	17.D	20.D	23.A
2.D	6.B	9.A	12.A	15.A	18.C	21.C	24.B
3.B	7.D	10.B	13.C	16.D	19.A	22.B	25.B
4.A							

TEST V. READING COMPREHENSION AND INTERPRETATION

1.D	4.C	7.C	10.A	12.A	14.B	16.A	18.B
2.A	5.D	8.D	11.E	13.A	15.D	17.C	19.C
3.D	6.A	9.B					

TEST VI. ARITHMETIC COMPUTATIONS

1.A	4.C	7.E	10.D	13.B
2.D	5.E	8.C	11.A	14.C
3.B	6.A	9.B	12.D	15.E

3

PART THREE

Judgment and Reasoning

ANSWER SHEET FOR INVESTIGATION QUIZZER

REASONING AND CRIMINOLOGY

1 Ⓐ Ⓑ Ⓒ Ⓓ	6 Ⓐ Ⓑ Ⓒ Ⓓ	11 Ⓐ Ⓑ Ⓒ Ⓓ	16 Ⓐ Ⓑ Ⓒ Ⓓ
2 Ⓐ Ⓑ Ⓒ Ⓓ	7 Ⓐ Ⓑ Ⓒ Ⓓ	12 Ⓐ Ⓑ Ⓒ Ⓓ	17 Ⓐ Ⓑ Ⓒ Ⓓ
3 Ⓐ Ⓑ Ⓒ Ⓓ	8 Ⓐ Ⓑ Ⓒ Ⓓ	13 Ⓐ Ⓑ Ⓒ Ⓓ	18 Ⓐ Ⓑ Ⓒ Ⓓ
4 Ⓐ Ⓑ Ⓒ Ⓓ	9 Ⓐ Ⓑ Ⓒ Ⓓ	14 Ⓐ Ⓑ Ⓒ Ⓓ	19 Ⓐ Ⓑ Ⓒ Ⓓ
5 Ⓐ Ⓑ Ⓒ Ⓓ	10 Ⓐ Ⓑ Ⓒ Ⓓ	15 Ⓐ Ⓑ Ⓒ Ⓓ	

FIREARMS

1 Ⓐ Ⓑ Ⓒ Ⓓ	6 Ⓐ Ⓑ Ⓒ Ⓓ	11 Ⓐ Ⓑ Ⓒ Ⓓ	16 Ⓐ Ⓑ Ⓒ Ⓓ
2 Ⓐ Ⓑ Ⓒ Ⓓ	7 Ⓐ Ⓑ Ⓒ Ⓓ	12 Ⓐ Ⓑ Ⓒ Ⓓ	17 Ⓐ Ⓑ Ⓒ Ⓓ
3 Ⓐ Ⓑ Ⓒ Ⓓ	8 Ⓐ Ⓑ Ⓒ Ⓓ	13 Ⓐ Ⓑ Ⓒ Ⓓ	18 Ⓐ Ⓑ Ⓒ Ⓓ
4 Ⓐ Ⓑ Ⓒ Ⓓ	9 Ⓐ Ⓑ Ⓒ Ⓓ	14 Ⓐ Ⓑ Ⓒ Ⓓ	19 Ⓐ Ⓑ Ⓒ Ⓓ
5 Ⓐ Ⓑ Ⓒ Ⓓ	10 Ⓐ Ⓑ Ⓒ Ⓓ	15 Ⓐ Ⓑ Ⓒ Ⓓ	

INVESTIGATIONS AND REPORTS

1 Ⓐ Ⓑ Ⓒ Ⓓ	4 Ⓐ Ⓑ Ⓒ Ⓓ	7 Ⓐ Ⓑ Ⓒ Ⓓ	10 Ⓐ Ⓑ Ⓒ Ⓓ	13 Ⓐ Ⓑ Ⓒ Ⓓ
2 Ⓐ Ⓑ Ⓒ Ⓓ	5 Ⓐ Ⓑ Ⓒ Ⓓ	8 Ⓐ Ⓑ Ⓒ Ⓓ	11 Ⓐ Ⓑ Ⓒ Ⓓ	14 Ⓐ Ⓑ Ⓒ Ⓓ
3 Ⓐ Ⓑ Ⓒ Ⓓ	6 Ⓐ Ⓑ Ⓒ Ⓓ	9 Ⓐ Ⓑ Ⓒ Ⓓ	12 Ⓐ Ⓑ Ⓒ Ⓓ	15 Ⓐ Ⓑ Ⓒ Ⓓ

EVIDENCE

1 Ⓐ Ⓑ Ⓒ Ⓓ	3 Ⓐ Ⓑ Ⓒ Ⓓ	5 Ⓐ Ⓑ Ⓒ Ⓓ	7 Ⓐ Ⓑ Ⓒ Ⓓ
2 Ⓐ Ⓑ Ⓒ Ⓓ	4 Ⓐ Ⓑ Ⓒ Ⓓ	6 Ⓐ Ⓑ Ⓒ Ⓓ	8 Ⓐ Ⓑ Ⓒ Ⓓ

INVESTIGATION QUIZZER

Investigations, regardless of type or ultimate purpose, involve gathering and evaluating information, and it is on this principle that the following questions have been selected.

DIRECTIONS: For each question in this test, read carefully the item and the four lettered choices that follow. Choose the answer which you consider correct or most nearly correct. Mark the answer sheet for the letter you have chosen, A, B, C, or D.

REASONING & CRIMINOLOGY

1. Of the following, the one which is least effective as an instrument for successfully combating the criminal is to
   (A) study criminal pathology
   (B) study the methods of the criminal
   (C) try to discover who the criminals are
   (D) ascertain how criminals operate.

2. "Correlation rather than compensation is the psychological rule." If correct this statement would indicate that a mentally defective prisoner whom you have arrested would probably be
   (A) compensatory rather than correlative
   (B) less adept at manual skills than a highly intelligent prisoner
   (C) correlative rather than compensatory
   (D) able to learn a skilled trade in prison more easily than a highly intelligent prisoner.

3. "In one study it was found that attitude toward the law is approximately the same for children in all social and economic conditions whether in city environment or in rural communities, and is but slightly different from that of adults." This finding serves most directly to indicate that
   (A) attitude toward the law is primarily a function of economic factors
   (B) persons who differ with regard to social and economic situation do not, in general differ with regard to attitude toward the law

   (C) the only difference between children and adults is one of chronological age
   (D) social and economic conditions are environmental products.

4. The least accurate characterization of crime is that it
   (A) consists of an overt act and, in most cases of a culpable intent
   (B) is an act prohibited by a group with the power to enforce observance
   (C) may be either an act of omission or commission
   (D) is an act which, generally of an illegal nature, is quite possibly legal in its essence.

5. The most effective method of crime prevention is in general
   (A) severe punishment of malefactors
   (B) probation
   (C) psychiatric examination of offenders
   (D) eradication of causal factors.

6. Of the following, the one which is a reason for believing prevention of criminal behavior to be superior to the cure of criminals as a method for handling crime problems is that with the adoption of preventive programs it is most probable that
   (A) less money will be spent on jails and prisons

(B) more money will be spent on preventive programs

(C) the "born" criminal will exhibit criminal behavior anyway

(D) less money will have to be spent on such matters as recreational programs, housing and the like.

7. If it is assumed that all criminals believe in no legal restraints then

(A) all persons who are not criminal believe in legal restraint

(B) any person who believes in no legal restraints is a criminal

(C) any person who does not believe in no legal restraints is not a criminal

(D) there would be no criminals if there were no legal restraints.

8. "It is an undeniable fact that people are not born criminals." Of the following, the chief implication of the above statement is that

(A) the youth who is a juvenile delinquent becomes the adult who violates the law

(B) violations of the law are usually due to a combination of environmental factors

(C) most crimes are committed by adults

(D) criminals are not easily detected.

9. "In the State of Delaware, public whipping is still employed as an official punishment for certain crimes." Solely on the basis of this statement, it is most accurate to infer that in Delaware

(A) crime is less frequent than in other states

(B) public whipping is considered an effective punishment

(C) some crimes are not considered to be as serious as they are in other states

(D) there have been few revisions of the penal code in modern times.

10. A businessperson requests advice concerning good practice in the use of a safe in the office. The one of the following points which should be stressed most in the use of safes is that

(A) a safe should not be placed where it can be seen from the street

(B) the combination should be written down and carefully hidden in the office

(C) a safe located in a dark place is more tempting to a burglar than one which is located in a well-lighted place

(D) factors of size and weight alone determine the protection offered by a safe.

11. A TV crime program dramatized a different police case every week, showed the capture or death of the criminal and ended with the slogan "Crime Does Not Pay." It was found that a gang of teen-age boys listened to this program every week in order to see what mistake was made by the criminal, and then duplicated the crime, trying to avoid the same mistake. This case illustrates that

(A) all criminal minds work the same way

(B) attempts to keep young people out of crime by frightening them into obeying the law are not always successful

(C) it is not possible to commit the perfect crime unless care is taken

(D) most criminals learn from their own mistakes.

12. "A criminal becomes either a thief, an assailant, or a sexual offender, never an all-around criminal." Of the following, an important reason for these basic differences in criminal behavior is probably that

(A) to be an all-around criminal requires more intelligence than the average criminal has

(B) crime syndicates have gained control over certain branches of crime and have made it difficult for a beginner to break in

(C) criminal acts are an expression of the criminal's whole personality

(D) most crimes are committed on the spur of the moment and without previous thought.

13. A young man who was arrested for smashing a store window and stealing a portable radio was asked why he did it. He answered: "Well, I wanted a radio and I just took it." If this answer is characteristic of the behavior of the young criminal, it is most reasonable to believe that

(A) the young criminal has a well-organized personality

(B) he sizes up each new situation in terms of his past experiences

(C) his decision to commit a crime is made after careful consideration of its possible effect on his future

(D) his temptation to commit a crime is an isolated situation, having, in his mind, little relation to his life as a whole.

(B) some criminals may be influenced to continue their careers of crime because they associate with other criminals

(C) the real motives for the commission of most crimes originate in punishment for criminal acts

(D) fear of imprisonment will make a criminal who has been in jail plan his second crime more carefully.

14. It is generally agreed that criminal tendencies are present in every person. A basic difference, however, between the normal person and the criminal is that the

(A) normal person sometimes commits trivial crimes but the criminal commits crimes of a major nature

(B) criminal is unable to understand the possible results of antisocial acts committed

(C) normal person is able to control antisocial tendencies and direct activities into socially approved channels

(D) criminal believes that he or she is no different from the person who does not commit crimes.

15. It has been claimed that a person who commits a crime sometimes has an unconscious wish to be punished, which is caused by strong unconscious feelings of guilt. The one of the following actions by a criminal which may be partly due to an unconscious desire for punishment is

(A) claiming that he or she doesn't know anything about the crime when questioned by the police

(B) accusing someone else when captured by the police

(C) revisiting the place where the crime was committed

(D) the care taken not to leave any clues at the scene of the crime.

16. "Experience has shown that many crimes have been planned in prison." From this finding, it is reasonable to assume that

(A) the principal motive for the commission of first crimes is the wish to take revenge on society

17. The general statistics of crime and criminals are known as the most unreliable and most difficult of all statistics. This unreliability results primarily from the fact that

(A) causal factors are variable in time and place

(B) differences in crime techniques make the collection of reliable statistics most difficult

(C) the amount of crime in any given jurisdiction at any given time cannot be accurately determined

(D) variations in recording techniques are such that comparisons on a common basis are almost impossible.

18. The following facts have been established by the investigator to prove that a certain person is a drug addict. Which of the statements is least consistent with the other three to show the suspect is a drug addict?

(A) He has a peculiar glistening look in his eyes

(B) He has been convicted of a crime

(C) Tests have disclosed intensification of the senses at various times

(D) He has shown symptoms of euphoria from time to time.

19. Mr. A is accused of counterfeiting U.S. Paper currency. Which of the following facts is most unfavorable to Mr. A, tending to strengthen the accusation?

(A) Five $20 bills have been found in his possession bearing the picture of President Jackson

(B) He had been convicted of bootlegging in the Prohibition era

(C) He was known in recent years to be a poor man, but he suddenly began to spend a lot of money on himself and his family

(D) Three months ago he inherited $500 from a distant relative.

Answer Key: Reasoning and Criminology

1. A	11. B
2. B	12. C
3. B	13. D
4. D	14. C
5. D	15. C
6. A	16. B
7. C	17. C
8. B	18. B
9. B	19. C
10. C	

FIREARMS

1. An escaped prisoner has been wounded and is lying flat on his stomach with his head turned to one side. The one of the following directions from which a trooper should approach the prisoner in order to make it most difficult for the prisoner to fire quickly and accurately at the trooper is from the side
    (A) directly behind the prisoner's head
    (C) facing the prisoner's face
    (B) facing the top of the prisoner's head
    (D) facing the prisoner's heels.

2. A trooper is investigating a complaint that a man is brandishing a gun in the rear of a restaurant at a time when customers are present. Of the following, the best reason for the trooper to exercise caution when entering is that
    (A) the man may open fire without warning and injure others
    (B) a trooper should not be exposed to dangerous risks
    (C) the man may injure himself
    (D) there may be a second exit from the room.

3. A trooper's suspicions are aroused that a man is carrying a concealed weapon. Upon being questioned, the man admits possession of a loaded revolver. He says that he has no license for the gun. However he informs the trooper he is on his way to contribute the gun to the army. Of the following, the best action for the trooper to take is to
    (A) arrest the man
    (B) congratulate the man for his patriotic deed
    (C) pretend to release the man, but follow him surreptitiously
    (D) take the gun and release the man, being careful first to take the man's name and address.

4. When starting to unload a revolver, it is safest to have the muzzle pointing
    (A) upward
    (B) downward
    (C) to the left
    (D) to the right.

5. The marks left on a bullet by a gun barrel are different from those left by any other gun barrel. This fact is most useful in directly identifying the
    (A) direction from which a shot was fired
    (B) person who fired a particular gun
    (C) gun from which a bullet was fired
    (D) bullet which caused a fatal wound.

6. The caliber of a gun is
    (A) its barrel length
    (B) the diameter of its barrel
    (C) the size of the ammunition used
    (D) neither (A), (B) or (C).

7. Identifying marks or imprints are not left on a shell by the
    (A) firing pin
    (B) ejector
    (C) extractor
    (D) hammer.

8. A very accurate test by which an expert can determine the distance from a bullet hole at which a gun was fired is called the
    (A) Alphanopthylamine test
    (B) Diphenylamine test
    (C) benzodine test
    (D) Photo-micrograph test.

9. Cannelure are valuable in firearms identification because they help the expert determine the
    (A) identity of the weapon that fired a particular bullet
    (B) type of gun that fired a particular bullet
    (C) manufacturer of the weapon
    (D) manufacturer of the bullet.

10. That part of the mechanism of a firearm that withdraws the shell or cartridge from the chamber is called the
    (A) extractor
    (B) ejector
    (C) primer
    (D) striker.

11. Pointing or aiming, intentionally but without malice, a firearm at or toward any person is classified in the Penal Law as
    (A) disorderly conduct
    (B) malicious mischief
    (C) a public nuisance
    (D) a crime involving public safety.

12. As a peace officer, you may be required to carry a revolver. Of the following, the *least* important rule for you to keep in mind concerning the handling and care of a revolver is to
    (A) point the revolver at somebody only if you actually intend to use it
    (B) check the revolver frequently to make certain that it is clean and well oiled
    (C) store the revolver, when you are not on duty, in an inaccessible place where children cannot possibly reach it
    (D) examine the revolver each time before you use it to make certain that it is loaded.

13. Uniformed officers are constantly urged to consider every revolver loaded until proven otherwise. Of the following, the best justification for this recommendation is that
    (A) there are many accidents involving apparently empty revolvers
    (B) police revolvers have safety devices
    (C) less danger is involved when facing armed thugs
    (D) ammunition deteriorates unless replaced periodically.

14. The proprietor of a tavern summons a trooper and turns over to him a loaded revolver that was found in one of the tavern's booths. Of the following, the least appropriate action for the trooper to take is to
    (A) close off the booth from use by other patrons
    (B) determine exactly when the revolver was found
    (C) obtain the names or descriptions of the persons who occupied the booth before the revolver was found
    (D) unload the gun and place it in an inside pocket.

15. Of the following, the best method to use in shooting a revolver is to keep
    (A) both eyes closed
    (B) both eyes open
    (C) the right eye open
    (D) the left eye open.

16. A state trooper is frequently advised to lie down before returning fire, if a person is shooting at him or her. This is primarily because
    (A) a smaller target will thus be presented to the assailant
    (B) the trooper can return the fire more quickly while in the prone position
    (C) the assailant will think he has struck the trooper and cease firing
    (D) it will indicate that the trooper is not the aggressor.

17. A trooper should fire a pistol
    (A) only as a last resort
    (B) at no time
    (C) primarily to inspire fear
    (D) to impress upon citizens the need for respect.

18. Suppose that a trooper, off duty and in civilian clothes, is visiting a county fair. The officer finds a loaded revolver on the ground near one of the exhibits. The trooper should
    (A) take the revolver to the lost and found department at the fair
    (B) retain the revolver temporarily while placing an advertisement in the lost and found columns of a daily newspaper
    (C) take the revolver to headquarters
    (D) take the revolver to one of the attendants.

19. A trooper observes several youths in the act of looting a gas station vending machine. The youths flee in several directions as he approaches, ignoring his order to halt. The trooper then shoots at them and they halt and are captured. The trooper's action was
    (A) right; it was the most effective way of capturing the criminals
    (B) wrong; extreme measures should not be taken in apprehending petty offenders
    (C) right; provided that there was no danger of shooting innocent bystanders
    (D) wrong; this is usually ineffective when more than one offender is involved.

INVESTIGATIONS AND REPORTS

1. A certain trooper usually avoids any expression of his personal opinions on morals, politics, or family relations when he is interviewing anyone in connection with an investigation. Such a policy is generally
   (A) bad, mainly because the investigator misses opportunities for finding things in common with the person being interviewed
   (B) good, mainly because the investigator's expressed opinions may influence the information offered by the person being interviewed
   (C) bad, mainly because the investigator's approach should be informal and frank rather than restrained
   (D) good, mainly because the interview will be speeded up.

2. You are beginning to question a boy whom you suspect of having stolen a car. The boy's father walks over and as you question the boy, the father answers every question before the boy has a chance to speak. On the basis of the behavior of the boy and his father, it is most reasonable to assume that
   (A) the boy is too frightened to talk
   (B) the father is trying to protect the boy
   (C) your method of questioning is not clear
   (D) your suspicions are not supported by the facts.

3. Of the following, the most important precaution for a trooper to observe before beginning work on a special assignment given to him by his supervisor is to see that
   (A) he fully understands the supervisor's instructions regarding the assignment
   (B) he knows precisely how long it will take him to complete the assignment
   (C) he understands fully the relationship of that assignment to the general function of his bureau
   (D) the assignment will not keep him too long from his regular work.

4. In making an investigation, which of the following procedures should be avoided:
   (A) reading the published standard works and the current literature on the subject
   (B) searching exclusively for facts the investigation expects to find
   (C) making use of special knowledge of others through personal interview and by correspondence

   (D) checking references and collateral information in footnotes and memorandas.

5. Which of the following statements regarding the preparation of an effective statement is the least likely to be considered a "must":
   (A) a joint statement must be drawn up if there is more than one informer
   (B) the informer must be thoroughly committed as to knowledge of the contents
   (C) the informer must not only sign the last page, but initial any additional pages
   (D) a statement must include the identity of the parties, the time and the place.

6. "Troopers must be careful in their inquiries not to endanger unnecessarily the reputation of any person who may be the subject of their investigation." According to this statement
   (A) an investigator who makes any unnecessary inquiries endangers his or her own reputation
   (B) a reputation for making thorough investigations should be carefully built up.
   (C) carelessness on the part of the trooper might harm the reputation of an innocent person
   (D) troopers are not allowed to ask questions that reflect upon anyone's reputation.

7. "The trooper's general plans for the investigation should be determined before starting on a case." Of the following, the best argument in favor of this procedure is that
   (A) a plan once adopted should not be modified unless there are very good reasons for doing so
   (B) steps in the investigation which duplicate each other or are of little value will be minimized
   (C) the plan for each investigation will be different
   (D) until an investigation is actually begun it is difficult to know the problems that will be encountered.

8. "A state trooper should never rely entirely on the data given by a witness." Of the following, the chief justification for this statement is the fact that
   (A) human perceptions are often incomplete and frequently affected by distortions
   (B) recall and recognition are apt to be more accurate when the passage of time has caused momentary passions and prejudices to cool

(C) a witness to an occurrence cannot always be found

(D) witnesses usually contradict each other.

9. A trooper's report always includes personal judgment on the credibility of the witnesses mentioned in the report. This practice is
   (A) desirable, mainly because it can be used to support the position that the investigator wants to take with respect to the case
   (B) undesirable, mainly because it is of no value to the reader of the report
   (C) desirable, mainly because it is part of the investigative function to evaluate the credibility of witnesses
   (D) undesirable, mainly because judgments should be formed on the basis of facts, not opinions.

10. Before you submit the written report of an investigation which you conducted, you become aware of some previously unknown information relating to the case. Your decision as to whether to re-write your report to include this additional information should be influenced mainly by the
    (A) amount of time remaining in which to submit the report
    (B) bearing this additional information will have on the findings and recommendations of the report
    (C) extent of the revision that will be required in the original report in order to include this additional information
    (D) feasibility of submitting a supplementary report at a later date.

11. "The most thorough investigation is of no value if the report written by the investigator does not enable the reader to readily decide the correct action to be taken." Of the following, the least direct implication of the preceding quotation is that the
    (A) investigation conducted must be very thorough to be of value
    (B) investigation report is generally written by the person who made the investigation
    (C) purpose of the investigation report is to give superiors a basis for action
    (D) worth of the investigation is affected by the report submitted.

12. For you to give your superior oral reports rather than written ones is
    (A) desirable; it will be easier for your superior to transmit your oral reports to his or her superiors
    (B) undesirable; the oral reports will provide no permanent record for reference
    (C) undesirable; there will be less opportunity for you to discuss the oral reports than the written ones
    (D) desirable; the oral reports will require little time and effort to prepare.

13. A trooper is frequently required to prepare various types of written reports. The one of the following features which is least desirable in a lengthy report is that
    (A) the style of writing should be readable, interesting, and impersonal; it should not be too scholarly, nor make use of involved sentence structure
    (B) recommendations and conclusions resulting from the facts incorporated in the body of the report must appear only at the end of the report so that readers can follow the writer's line of reasoning
    (C) in determining the extent of technical detail and terminology to be used in the presentation of supporting data, such as charts, tables, graphs, case examples, etc., the technical knowledge of the prospective reader or readers should be kept in mind
    (D) the body of the report should mention all the pertinent facts and develop the writer's ideas in such a way that the recommendations will be a logical outgrowth of the arguments presented.

14. "Troopers are required to submit written reports of all unusual occurrences." Of the following, the best justification for making written notes as soon as possible after the unusual occurrence is that
    (A) the experienced trooper has had long experience with and can easily handle all types of unusual occurrences
    (B) reports written after a long delay tend to be excessively long
    (C) proper perspective of an incident increases with the passage of time
    (D) memory of specific events is more accurate when the event is fresh in mind.

15. It is important that a trooper be able to use correct grammatical construction in writing official reports chiefly because
    (A) most officers are able to write grammatically

(B) intelligent people tend to use good grammar
(C) use of incorrect grammar may lead to misinterpretation
(D) many reports are used only for statistical purposes.

EVIDENCE

1. In the collection and preparaton of evidence to be presented in court, the investigator should remember that the presumption of the court concerning the origin of the fire is
   (A) that a criminal agency was responsible for the cause of the burning
   (B) that when a building is burned it is the result of accident
   (C) that a confession made out of court by the accused is sufficient proof of the motive
   (D) that a building which was burned has been wilfully fired by some responsible person.

2. In the consideration of confessions the general rule is for the court to presume that
   (A) a confession is usually involuntary and the plaintiff must show that it was not
   (B) the threat, promise or inducement used to obtain a confession influenced the defendant to tell the story
   (C) a confession is voluntary and the burden is on the defendant to show that it was not
   (D) the jury alone can determine whether the confession was voluntary or involuntary

3. A confession by a person accused of a crime tends to prove guilt only if it is
   (A) uncontradicted
   (B) made before a judicial office
   (C) not corroborated by other evidence
   (D) signed by the accused.

4. A valid confession consists of
   (A) a voluntary declaration that the charge or allegation made is correct
   (B) a plea of former acquittal of the offense charged
   (C) a statement made in contemplation of death
   (D) an acknowledgment of admission, under duress, of the alleged facts.

5. Hearsay evidence is useful to an investigator
   (A) as evidence at a hearing

(B) only as circumstantial evidence
(C) as a basis for securing real evidence
(D) as a basis upon which to secure a conviction.

6. The one of the following sources of evidence which would be most likely to give information needed to verify residence, is
   (A) family affidavits
   (B) medical and hospital bills
   (C) an original birth certificate
   (D) rental receipts.

7. The principal reason why the courts require that a confession be voluntary before it can be admitted as evidence is that
   (A) confessions seldom reveal the whole truth
   (B) the information contained in a confession cannot be corroborated by factual evidence
   (C) confessions are at best only circumstantial evidence
   (D) an involuntary confession constitutes a denial of a person's constitutional right to a fair trial.

8. The first essential to the admissibility of all evidence is that it must
   (A) tend to prove the guilt of the defendant
   (B) be logically relevant
   (C) be attested to by more than one witness
   (D) be an admission against interest.

Answer Key : Firearms

1. A	5. C	9. D	13. A	17. A
2. A	6. D	10. A	14. D	18. C
3. A	7. D	11. D	15. B	19. B
4. B	8. D	12. D	16. A	

Answer Key : Reports

1. B	5. A	9. C	13. B
2. B	6. C	10. B	14. D
3. A	7. B	11. A	15. C
4. B	8. A	12. B	

Answer Key : Evidence

1. B	3. A	5. C	7. D
2. C	4. A	6. D	8. B

JUDGMENT FOR LAW ENFORCEMENT OFFICERS

1. "One can only see what one observes and one observes only things which are already in the mind." Of the following, the chief implication of this statement is that
   (A) observation, to be most effective, should be directed and conscious
   (B) all aspects of a situation, unless the law enforcement officer exercises caution, are likely to strike him with equal forcefulness
   (C) observation should be essentially indirect if it is to be accurate
   (D) memory is essentially perception one step removed from observation.

2. "The number of arrests made is not always the best indication of a successful state trooper." The statement most consistent with the above quotation is that
   (A) a number of factors should be considered in properly evaluating the performance of a trooper
   (B) there is a negative correlation between the number of arrests made and the success of a trooper
   (C) state troopers should avoid making arrests whenever possible
   (D) the success of a state trooper cannot be precisely and objectively measured.

3. A law enforcement officer is in the habit in his free time of occasionally inventing imaginary law enforcement problems on his post and attempting to provide appropriate solutions to these happenings. This sort of behavior is best characterized as
   (A) undesirable, since it may lead to insanity
   (B) desirable, since it exercises the mind
   (C) desirable, since he may, as a result, be better prepared for emergencies
   (D) undesirable, in that his attention is less readily given to what is actually happening on his post.

4. "Training produces co-operation and brings about lower unit costs of operation." According to this statement, it is most logical to assume that
   (A) a program of personnel training is a major feature of every large business organization
   (B) training is a factor in improving morale and efficiency
   (C) training is of more value to new workers than to old employees
   (D) unless personnel costs can be lowered, training is of little value.

5. As an intelligent law enforcement officer, you should know that, of the following, the one which is least likely to be followed by an increase in crime is
   (A) war
   (C) poor housing
   (B) depression
   (D) prosperity.

6. Law enforcement officials receive badges with numbers on them so that
   (A) their personalities may be submerged
   (B) they may be more easily identified
   (C) they may be spied upon
   (D) their movements may be kept under constant control.

7. If you were asked what you thought of a person you didn't know, what should you say?
   (A) I will go and get acquainted
   (B) I think that person is all right
   (C) I don't know the person and can't say
   (D) I think the person is worthless.

8. The best attitude for a trooper to take is to
   (A) be constantly on the alert
   (B) be hostile

(C) vary watchfulness with the apparent necessity for it

(D) regard tact as the most effective weapon for handling any degree of disorder.

9. A trooper who has been assigned to work with you has a receding chin. It is most probably that he will
   (A) be most like the other troopers in your group
   (B) lack will power to a marked degree
   (C) be a very timid person
   (D) constantly carry tales to you about the other officers.

10. The annual number of arrests recorded in Area A is 1,000. The annual number of arrests recorded in Area B is 1,200. It is safe to infer from this information
   (A) that there are more criminals in Area A than in Area B
   (B) that more persons are imprisoned in Area A than in Area B
   (C) there is more disrespect for law in Area A than in Area B
   (D) none of the foregoing.

11. Ten percent of the inmates released from a certain prison are arrested as parole violators. It follows that
   (A) 90 percent have reformed
   (B) 10 percent have reformed
   (C) none have reformed
   (D) none of the foregoing is necessarily true.

12. It has been stated that arrests are made in only 44 percent of the crimes committed, while only 40 percent of those arrested are convicted. The most reasonable inference from these data is that
   (A) most criminal acts are not immediately followed by the arrest of the criminal
   (B) a small number of persons are arrested
   (C) most of those persons who are arrested are also convicted
   (D) people without influence are most likely to be convicted after arrest.

13. An insane person who has a wife and two children is arrested on a charge of burglary. It follows from these data that
   (A) we have here insufficient information from

which to draw any conclusions with reference to the relation between crime and insanity
   (B) burglary is a crime which attracts lunatics
   (C) this proves that not all lunatics are burglars
   (D) a burglar is one type of lunatic.

14. A certain committee found that over 90 percent of the murders in the United States are committed by use of pistols. It follows that
   (A) almost all murders are caused by the possession of pistols
   (B) 90 percent of murders can be eliminated by eliminating the sale and use of pistols
   (C) the pistol is a mechanical aid to crime
   (D) no information is available with regard to the way murders happen.

15. **The causes of crime**
   (A) are exactly the same today as in the past
   (B) have been accurately and completely determined
   (C) are an unimportant matter
   (D) are an extremely complicated problem.

16. **A criminal is typically one who**
   (A) has a peculiarly shaped head
   (B) exhibits a most degenerate kind of behavior
   (C) is an intelligent, well educated person
   (D) looks like other people.

There would be no crime if there were no
   (A) weapons
   (B) criminals
   (C) stupid laws
   (D) private property.

18. A trooper receives instructions from the supervisor which he does not fully understand. For the trooper to ask for a further explanation would be
   (A) good; chiefly because the supervisor will be impressed with his interest in his work.
   (B) poor; chiefly because the time of the supervisor will be needlessly wasted
   (C) good; chiefly because proper performance depends on full understanding of the work to be done
   (D) poor; chiefly because officers should be able to think for themselves.

19. The FBI reports that the crime rate in New Jersey in one year was 10.6 percent higher than in the previous year, while the average increase in crime throughout the United States was 7.6 percent. It may logically be concluded from these facts that
   (A) most New Jersey residents have lost their respect for the law
   (B) New Jersey police officials are more conscientious than those of other states
   (C) New Jersey's laws are more severe than those of other states
   (D) New Jersey's increased crime rate may be due to a combination of reasons not listed above.

20. The one of the following statements concerning the behavior of law enforcement officers which is most accurate is
   (A) a show of confident assurance on the part of a law enforcement officer will make it possible to cover a shortage of knowledge in any given duty
   (B) in ordinary cases, when a newly appointed officer does not know what to do, it is always better to do too much than to do too little
   (C) it is not advisable that officers recommend the employment of certain attorneys for individuals taken into custody
   (D) a prisoner who is morose and refuses to talk will bear less watching by an officer than one who threatens to kill himself.

21. A law enforcement officer should know that character can be influenced only when and in so far as
   (A) the desire for ideals has been aroused
   (B) a knowledge of principles of conduct has been acquired
   (C) problems of behavior have been clearly defined
   (D) plans for meeting specific situations are carried into conduct.

22. In dealing with children a law enforcement officer should always
   (A) treat them the same as adults
   (B) instill in them a fear of the law
   (C) secure their confidence
   (D) impress them with the right of the law to punish them for wrong-doing.

23. Of the following, the greatest danger in arming a trooper detailed to guard prisoners in hospitals is that
   (A) the gun may accidentally go off, wounding prisoners and others within gunshot
   (B) the trooper may use the gun without adequate cause
   (C) the prisoners may disarm the trooper
   (D) it is hazardous to permit too many people to possess firearms.

24. Charging a fee for fortune-telling is not permitted under the laws of this State. In spite of this, fortune-telling in various forms remains popular. Of the following, the least likely reason for this popularity is that many people
   (A) fear to make their own decisions in important matters
   (B) have such drab lives that they must search for a hope of change
   (C) wish to use fortune-tellers for entertainment at their social gatherings
   (D) wish to make contacts with loved ones who have died.

25. The one of the following which is the most probable reason for the considerably increasing proportion of serious crimes committed by women is
   (A) that the proportion of women in the population is increasing
   (B) that greater supervision of women results in a greater number of arrests
   (C) the success of women in achieving social equality with men
   (D) the increasing number of crime stories in the movies and on television.

26. "Undoubtedly the most important influence upon the growing youngster is wielded by the adults whom he or she observes day after day." Accordingly, the type of adult behavior that generally would be least likely to adversely affect youngsters is
   (A) dishonesty by public officials
   (B) lack of courtesy in the home
   (C) intolerance in the school
   (D) racial discrimination in the neighborhood youth club.

27 It frequently happens that a major crime of an unusual nature is followed almost immediately

by an "epidemic" of several crimes, in widely scattered locations, which have elements similar to the first one. Of the following, the most likely explanation for this situation is that
(A) the same criminal is likely to commit the same type of a crime
(B) a gang of criminals will operate in several areas simultaneously
(C) newspaper publicity on a major crime is apt to influence other would-be criminals
(D) the same causes which are responsible for the first crime are also responsible for the others.

28. "A member of the department shall not indulge in intoxicants while in uniform. A member of the department not required to wear a uniform and a uniformed member while out of uniform shall not indulge in intoxicants to an extent unfitting him or her for duty." It follows that a
(A) member off duty, not in uniform, may drink intoxicants to any degree desired
(B) member not on duty, in uniform, may drink intoxicants
(C) member on duty, not in uniform, may drink intoxicants.
(D) uniformed member, in civilian clothes, may not drink intoxicants.

29. The reason state trooper have greater authority than private citizens in making arrests is
(A) to protect citizens against needless arrest
(B) to insure a fair trial
(C) that they have greater knowledge of the law
(D) that they are in better physical shape.

30. "The treatment to be given the offender cannot alter the fact of his offense; but we can take measures to reduce the chances of similar acts in the future. We should banish the criminal, not in order to exact revenge nor directly to encourage reform but to deter him and others from further illegal attacks on society." According to this paragraph, the principal reason for punishing criminals is to
(A) prevent the commission of future crimes
(B) remove them safely from society
(C) avenge society
(D) teach them that crime does not pay.

31. "The law enforcement officer's art consists in applying and enforcing a multitude of laws and ordinances in such degree or proportion and in such manner that the greatest degree of social protection will be secured. The degree of enforcement and the method of application will vary with each neighborhood and community." According to the foregoing paragraph
(A) each neighborhood or community must judge for itself to what extent the law is to be enforced
(B) a law enforcement officer should only enforce those laws which are designed to give the greatest degree of social protection
(C) the manner and intensity of law enforcement is not necessarily the same in all
(D) all laws and ordinances must be enforced in a community with the same degree of intensity.

32. It is well known that many criminals in the city
(A) belong to subversive organizations
(B) work at respectable jobs during the day
(C) are professionally trained
(D) live in crowded localities.

33. When arrested, boys under 16 are not brought to the same place of detention as older ones. The reason for this separation is most likely to
(A) keep them with others of their own age
(B) protect them from rough police methods
(C) help them get sound legal aid
(D) keep them from contact with hardened criminals.

Law Enforcement Judgment: Answer Key

1. A	6. B	11. D	16. D	21. A	26. A	31. C
2. A	7. C	12. A	17. B	22. C	27. C	32. D
3. C	8. A	13. A	18. C	23. C	28. C	33. D
4. B	9. A	14. C	19. D	24. C	29. A	
5. D	10. D	15. D	20. C	25. C	30. A	

4

PART FOUR

Reading and Reporting

TEN SUCCESS STEPS IN READING INTERPRETATION

Here are proven techniques for getting the right
answer to *any* Reading Interpretation question.

Survey Selection

1. Read the selection through quickly to get the
general sense.
2. Reread the selection, concentrating on the central idea.
3. Can you now pick out the *topic sentence* in
each paragraph?
4. If the selection consists of more than one paragraph, determine the *central idea* of the entire
selection.

Survey Stems
Concentrate on Each Question

5. Examine the five choices carefully, yet rapidly.
Eliminate immediately those choices which are *far-fetched, ridiculous, irrelevant, false,* or *impossible.*
6. Eliminate those choices which may be true, but
which have nothing to do with the sense of the
selection.
7. Check those few choices which now remain as
possibilities.

Reread Selectively
Shuttle Back to Selection

8. Refer back to the original selection and determine which one of these remaining possibilities
is best in view of

a) specific information in the selection
or
b) implied information in the selection

Reread only the part of the selection that applies
to the question, and make your decision as to the
correct choice based on these considerations:

(a) A choice must be based on fact actually
given or definitely understood (and not on your
personal opinion or prejudice.) Some questions require making a judgment—and this judgment also
must be based on the facts as given.

(b) In questions involving the central thought
of the passage (for example: "The best title for
this selection . . .") the choice must accurately
reflect the entire thought—not too narrow, and not
too general.

9. Be sure to consider only the facts *given* or
definitely understood some place in the selection.

10. Be especially careful of trick expressions or
"catch-words" which sometimes destroy the validity
of a seemingly acceptable answer. These include
the expressions: "under all circumstances," "at all
times," "never," "always," "under no conditions,"
"absolutely," "completely," and "entirely."

AVOID THE TRAPS

Trap #1—Sometimes the question cannot
be answered on the basis of the stated facts.
You may be required to make a deduction
from the facts given.
Trap #2—Eliminate your personal opinions.

Trap #3—Search out significant details that
are nestled in the paragraph. Reread the
paragraph as many times as necessary (with
an eye on your watch).

POLICE WORK READING QUIZZER

DIRECTIONS: Below each of the following passages you will find one or more incomplete statements about the passage. Select the words or expressions that most satisfactorily complete each statement in accordance with the meaning of the paragraph. Record your answers on a separate piece of paper.

1. "The trooper's art consists in applying and enforcing a multitude of laws and ordinances in such degree or proportion and in such manner that the greatest degree of social protection will be secured. The degree of enforcement and the method of application will vary with each neighborhood and community." According to the foregoing paragraph
   (A) each neighborhood or community must judge for itself to what extent the law is to be enforced
   (B) a trooper should only enforce those laws which are designed to give the greatest degree of social protection
   (C) the manner and intensity of law enforcement is not necessarily the same in all communities
   (D) all laws and ordinances must be enforced in a community with the same degree of intensity.

2. "Police control in the sense of regulating the details of police operations involves such matters as the technical means for so organizing the available personnel that competent police leadership, when secured, can operate effectively. It is concerned not so much with the extent to which popular controls can be trusted to guide and direct the course of police protection as with the administrative relationships which should exist between the component parts of the police organism." According to the foregoing statement, police control is
   (A) solely a matter of proper personnel assignment
   (B) the means employed to guide and direct the course of police protection
   (C) principally concerned with the administrative relationships between units of a police organization
   (D) the sum total of means employed in rendering police protection.

3. "As a rule, troopers, through service and experience, are familiar with the duties and the methods and means required to perform

them. Yet, left to themselves, their aggregate effort would disintegrate and the vital work of preserving the peace would never be accomplished." According to this paragraph, the most accurate of the following conclusions is
   (A) troopers are sufficiently familiar with their duties to need no supervision
   (B) working together for a common purpose is not efficient without supervision
   (C) troopers are familiar with the methods of performing their duties because of rules
   (D) preserving the peace is so vital that it can never be said to be completed.

4. "The number of arrests made is not always the best indication of a successful peace officer." The statement most consistent with the above quotation is that
   (A) a number of factors should be considered in properly evaluating the performance of a peace officer
   (B) there is a negative correlation between the number of arrests and an officer's success
   (C) troopers should avoid making arrests whenever possible
   (D) an officer's success cannot be precisely and objectively measured.

Answer questions 5 through 7 on the basis of the following paragraph:

"Criminal science is largely the science of identification. Progress in this field has been marked and sometimes very spectacular because new techniques, instruments and facts flow continuously from the scientists. But the crime laboratories are undermanned, trade secrets still prevail and inaccurate conclusions are often the result. However, modern gadgets cannot substitute for the skilled intelligent investigator; he must be their master."

5. According to this paragraph, criminal science
   (A) excludes the field of investigation
   (B) is primarily interested in establishing identity

(C) is based on the equipment used in crime laboratories

(D) uses techniques different from those used in other sciences.

6. Advances in criminal science have been, according to the paragraph,
   (A) extremely limited
   (B) slow but steady
   (C) unusually reliable
   (D) outstanding.

7. A problem that has not been overcome completely in crime work is, according to the paragraph,
   (A) unskilled investigators
   (B) the expense of new equipment and techniques
   (C) an insufficient number of personnel in crime laboratories
   (D) inaccurate equipment used in laboratories.

Answer questions 8 through 11 solely on the basis of the following paragraph:

"Automobile tire tracks found at the scene of a crime constitute an important link in the chain of physical evidence. In many cases, these are the only clues available. In some areas, unpaved ground adjoins the highway or paved streets. A suspect will often park a car off the paved portion of the street when committing a crime, sometimes leaving excellent tire tracks. Comparison of the tire track impressions with the tire is possible only when the vehicle has been found. However, the initial problem facing the police is the task of determining what kind of car probably made the impressions found at the scene of the crime. If the make, model and year of the car which made the impressions can be determined, it is obvious that the task of elimination is greatly lessened."

8. The one of the following which is the most appropriate title for the above paragraph is
   (A) The Use of Automobiles in the Commission of Crimes
   (B) The Use of Tire Tracks in Police Work
   (C) The Capture of Criminals by Scientific Police Work
   (D) The Positive Identification of Criminals Through Their Cars.

9. When searching for clear signs left by the car used in the commision of a crime, the most likely place for the police to look would be on the
   (A) highway adjoining unpaved streets
   (B) highway adjacent to paved street
   (C) paved street adjacent to the highway

(D) unpaved ground adjacent to a highway.

10. Automobile tire tracks found at the scene of a crime are of value as evidence in that they are
    (A) generally sufficient to trap and convict a suspect
    (B) the most important link in the chain of physical evidence
    (C) often the only evidence at hand
    (D) circumstantial rather than direct.

11. The primary reason for the police to try to find out which make, model and year of car was involved in the commission of a crime is to
    (A) compare the tire tracks left at the scene of the crime with the type of tires used on cars of that make
    (B) determine if the mud on the tires of the suspected car matches the mud in the unpaved road near the scene of the crime
    (C) reduce to a large extent the amount of work involved in determining the particular car used in the commission of a crime
    (D) alert the police patrol forces to question the occupants of all automobiles of this type.

Answer Questions 12 through 15 solely on the basis of the following paragraph:

"When stopping vehicles on highways to check for suspects or fugitives, the police use an automobile roadblock whenever possible. This consists of three cars placed in prearranged positions. Car number one is parked across the left lane of the roadway with the front diagonally facing toward the center line. Car number two is parked across the right lane, with the front of the vehicle also toward the center line, in a position perpendicular to car number one and approximately twenty feet to the rear. Continuing another twenty feet to the rear along the highway, car number three is parked in an identical manner to car number one. The width of the highway determines the angle or position in which the autos should be placed. In addition to the regular roadblock signs, and the use of flares at night only, there is an officer located at both the entrance and exit to direct and control traffic from both directions. This type of roadblock forces all approaching autos to reduce speed and zigzag around the police cars. Officers standing behind the parked cars can most safely and carefully view all passing motorists. Once a suspect is inside the block it becomes extremely difficult to crash out."

12. Of the following, the most appropriate title for this paragraph is
    (A) The Construction of an Escape-Proof

Roadblock.
(B) Regulation of Automobile Traffic Through a Police Roadblock
(C) Safety Precautions Necessary in Making an Automobile Roadblock
(D) Structure of a Roadblock to Detain Suspects or Fugitives.

13. When setting up a three-car roadblock, the relative positions of the cars should be such that
(A) the front of car number one is placed diagonally to the center line and faces car number three
(B) car number three is placed parallel to the center line and its front faces the right side of the road
(C) car number two is placed about 20 feet from car number one and its front faces the left side of the road
(D) car number three is parallel to and about 20 feet away from car number one.

14. Officers can observe occupants of all cars passing through the roadblock with greatest safety when
(A) warning flares are lighted to illuminate the area sufficiently at night
(B) warning signs are put up at each end of the roadblock
(C) they are stationed at both the exit and the entrance of the roadblock
(D) they take up positions behind cars in the roadblock.

15. The type of automobile roadblock described in the above paragraph is of value in police work because
(A) a suspect is unable to escape its confines by using force
(B) it is frequently used to capture suspects with no danger to the police
(C) it requires only two officers to set up and operate
(D) vehicular traffic within its confines is controlled as to speed and direction.

Answer Questions 16 and 17 solely on the basis of the following paragraph:

"Proper firearms training is one phase of law enforcement which cannot be ignored. No part of the training of a police officer is more important or more valuable. The officer's life and often the lives of fellow officers depend directly upon skill with the weapon he or she is carrying. Proficiency with the revolver is not attained exclusively by the volume of ammunition used and the number of hours spent on the firing line. Supervised practice and the use of training aids and techniques help make the shooter. It is essential to have a good firing range where new officers are trained and older personnel practice in scheduled firearms sessions. The fundamental points to be stressed are grip, stance, breathing, sight alignment and trigger squeeze. Coordination of thought, vision and motion must be achieved before the officer gains confidence in shooting ability. Attaining this ability will make the student a better officer and enhance his or her value to the force."

16. A police officer will gain confidence in shooting ability only after he or she has
(A) spent the required number of hours on the firing line
(B) been given sufficient supervised practice
(C) learned the five fundamental points
(D) learned to coordinate revolver movement with sight and thought.

17. Proper training in the use of firearms is one aspect of law enforcement which must be given serious consideration chiefly because it is the
(A) most useful and essential single factor in the training of a police officer
(B) one phase of police officer training which stresses mental and physical coordination
(C) costliest aspect of police officer training, involving considerable expense for the ammunition used in target practice
(D) most difficult part of police officer training.

18. "The large number of fatal motor-vehicle accidents renders necessary organization of special units in the department to cope with the technical problems encountered in such investigations." The generalization which can be inferred most directly from this statement is that
(A) large problems require specialists
(B) technical problems require specialists
(C) many trooper problems require special handing
(D) many troopers are specialists
(E) the number of motor-vehicle accidents which are fatal is large.

Answer Questions 19 to 22 solely on the basis of the following paragraph:

It is not always understood that the term "physical evidence" embraces any and all objects, living or inanimate. A knife, gun, signature or burglar tool is immediately recognized as physical evidence. Less often is it considered that dust, microscopic fragments of all types, even an odor, may equally be physical evidence and often the most important of all. It is well established that the most useful types of physical evidence are generally microscopic in dimensions, that is, not noticeable by the eye and therefore most likely to be overlooked by the criminal and by the investigator. For this reason microscopic evidence persists for months or years after all other evidence has been removed and found inconclusive. Naturally, there are limitations to the time of collecting miscroscopic evidence as it may be lost or decayed. The exercise of judgment as to the possibility or profit of delayed action in collecting the evidence is a field in which the expert investigator should judge.

19. The one of the following which the above paragraph does *not* consider to be physical evidence is a
   (A) criminal thought
   (B) minute speck of dust
   (C) raw onion smell
   (D) typewritten note.

20. According to the above paragraph, the rechecking of the scene of a crime
   (A) is useless when performed years after the occurrence of the crime
   (B) is advisable chiefly in crimes involving physical violence
   (C) may turn up microscopic evidence of value
   (D) should be delayed if the microscopic evidence is not subject to decay or loss.

21. According to the above paragraph, the criminal investigator should
   (A) give most attention to weapons used in the commission of the crime
   (B) ignore microscopic evidence until a request is received from the laboratory
   (C) immediately search for microscopic evidence and ignore the more visible objects
   (D) realize that microscopic evidence can be easily overlooked.

22. According to the above paragraph,
   (A) a delay in collecting evidence must definitely diminish its value to the investigator
   (B) microscopic evidence exists for longer periods of time than other physical evidence
   (C) microscopic evidence is generally the most useful type of physical evidence
   (D) physical evidence is likely to be overlooked by the criminal and by the investigator.

Answer questions 23 to 25 solely on the basis of the following paragraph:

"The crime laboratory performs a valuable service in crime investigation by assisting in the reconstruction of criminal action and by aiding in the identification of persons and things. When studied by a technician, physical things found at crime scenes often reveal facts useful in identifying the criminal and in determining what has occurred. The nature of substances to be examined and the character of the examinations to be made vary so widely that the services of a large variety of skilled scientific persons are needed in crime investigations. To employ such a complete staff and to provide them with equipment and standards needed for all possible analyses and comparisons is beyond the means and the needs of any but the largest departments. The search of crime scenes for physical evidence also calls for the services of specialists supplied with essential equipment and assigned to each tour of duty so as to provide service at any hour."

23. If a department employs a large staff of various types in its laboratory, it will affect crime investigation to the extent that
   (A) most crimes will be speedily solved
   (B) identification of criminals will be aided
   (C) search of crime scenes for physical evidence will become of less importance
   (D) investigation by police officers will not usually be required.

24. According to this paragraph, the most complete study of objects found at the scenes of crimes is
   (A) always done in all departments
   (B) based on assigning one technician to each tour of duty
   (C) probably done only in large departments
   (D) probably done in departments of states with low crime rates.

25. According to this paragraph, a large variety of skilled technicians is useful in criminal investigations because
   (A) crimes cannot be solved without their assistance as part of the investigation team
   (B) large departments need large staffs
   (C) many different kinds of tests on various substances can be made.
   (D) the state police cannot predict what methods may be tried by wily criminals.

Answer Key

1.C	6.D	11.C	16.D	21.D
2.C	7.C	12.D	17.A	22.C
3.B	8.B	13.C	18.B	23.B
4.A	9.D	14.D	19.A	24.C
5.B	10.C	15.D	20.C	25.C

READING QUESTIONS ON ROUTINES

DIRECTIONS: Below each of the following passages you will find one or more incomplete statements about the passage. Select the words or expressions that most satisfactorily complete each statement in accordance with the meaning of the paragraph.

Questions 1 to 10 relate to the report of an accident. Under "A" you are given the regulations governing filling out the report form. Under "B" you are given the completed report upon the basis of which you are to answer the questions.

"A"—1. A report form will be filled out for each person injured.

2. Be brief, but do not omit any information which can help the Department reduce number of accidents. If it is necessary, use more than one card.

3. Under "Details" enter all important facts not reported elsewhere on the card, which may be pertinent to the completeness of the report as: the specific traffic violation, if any; whether the injured person was crossing not at crossing; crossing against lights; the direction the vehicle was proceeding and if making right or left turn; attending surgeon; etc. If the officer is an eye witness he should be able to determine the cause.

"B"—Report:
INJURED PERSON: John C. Witherspoon; SEX: Male; AGE: 52
ADDRESS: 2110 Fairwell Road, Austin, Tx.
PLACE OF OCCURRENCE: 72nd Street and Broadway; DATE: 3.12.82.
ACCIDENT: Yes; NO. OF PERSONS INVOLVED: 12; TIME: 10 a.m.
NATURE OF INJURY: Right forearm, fractured
STRUCK BY: Auto No. 3
DRIVER INVOLVED:

Auto 1. Helmut Baldman 11 Far Street—Lic. 2831 owner

Auto 2. John Dunn 106 Near Ave.—Lic. 1072 owner

Auto 3. Robert Payne 32 Open Road—Lic. 666 owner

DETAILS: (1) Vehicle 1 came out of 72nd Street just as the lights along 72nd Street were changing to green going west. (2) Vehicle 2 proceding north north along Broadway continuied across the intersection as the lights in his direction turned red. (3) Vehicle 1 colliding with Vehicle 2 turning said vehicle over and throwing it into the path of Vehicle 3 going east along 72nd Street. (4) This had manifold results: other vehicles were struck; a hydrant was obliterated; several pedestrians were injured; there was considerible property damage; and three riders in the cars involved were killed. (5) This was a very tragic accident.

1. In the report, the one of the following words which was misspelled is
   (A) fractured
   (B) owner
   (C) vehicle
   (D) proceding.

2. In the report, the one of the following words which was misspelled is
   (A) continuied
   (B) across
   (C) intersection
   (D) colliding.

3. Why is this accident report being filed by a Texas Ranger even though the accident occurred on a city street?
   (A) the Ranger was the first officer on the scene
   (B) the officer felt like it
   (C) no one else wanted to do it since it was such a minor incident
   (D) state troopers are, in many states, held responsible for traffic control and law en-

forcement around the capital area in state capitals.

4. In the report, the one of the following words which was used incorrectly is
   (A) manifold
   (B) obliterated
   (C) intersection
   (D) fractured.

5. In the report, under "Details" there are several errors in grammar. Of the changes listed below, a change which will correct an existing error in grammar is
   (A) Change sentence (1) to, "Vehicle 1, going west, came out of 72nd Street just as the lights along 72nd Street were changing to green."
   (B) Change sentence (2) to, "Vehicle 2 proceded north along Broadway continuied across the intersection as the lights in his direction turned red."
   (C) Change sentence (3) to, "Vehicle 1 colliding with vehicle 2 turns said vehicle over and throwing it into the path of vehicle 3 going east along 72nd St."
   (D) Change sentence (4) to, "This has had manifold results: there was considerible property damage; a hydrant was obliterated; and several pedestrians were injured."

6. A change which will correct an existing error in grammar is
   (A) Change sentence (1) to, "Vehicle 1 came out of 72nd St. just as the lights along 72nd Street changed to green going west."
   (B) Change sentence (2) to, "Vehicle 2 proceding north along Broadway continuied across the intersection when the light in his direction turned red."
   (C) Change sentence (3) to, "Vehicle 1 collided with vehicle 2 turning said vehicle over and throwing it into the path of vehicle 3 going east along 72nd Street."
   (D) Change all semicolons in sentence (4) to commas.

7. Of the following critical evaluations of the report, the most correct is that it is a
   (A) Good report; it gives a graphic description of the accident
   (B) Bad report; the damage to the car is not given in detail

   (C) Bad report; it does not indicate, in detail, the cause of Witherspoon's injury
   (D) Bad report; there is no indication of what happened to the 11 persons other than Witherspoon who were involved.

8. Of the following, the report indicates most clearly
   (A) that some city property was damaged
   (B) that Witherspoon was a pedestrian
   (C) that the reporting officer was an eye witness
   (D) the names of all the drivers involved.

9. Of the following, the report indicates least clearly
   (A) the time of the accident
   (B) the direction in which Baldman was driving
   (C) how the accident might have been avoided
   (D) the number of persons involved.

10. From the report, as submitted, it is most reasonable to infer that
    (A) Baldman was at fault
    (B) the information is too hazy to determine the guilty person
    (C) Dunn was at fault
    (D) the accident was the fault of no one person.

Answer questions 11 to 13 solely on the basis of the following paragraph:

"All members of the state police force must recognize that the people, through their representatives, hire and pay them and that, as in any other employment, there must exist a proper employer-employee relationship. The state police officer must understand that the essence of a correct police attitude is a willingness to serve, but at the same time, should distinguish between service and servility, and between courtesy and softness. He or she must be firm but also courteous, avoiding even an appearance of rudeness. He or she should develop a position that is friendly and unbiased, pleasant and sympathetic, in relations with the general public, but firm and impersonal on occasions calling for regulation and control. A state police officer should understand that the primary purpose is to prevent violations, not to arrest people. He or she should recognize the line of demarcation between a police function and passing judgment which is a court function. On the other side, a public that cooperates with the state police, that supports them in their efforts and that observes laws and regulations may be said to have a desirable attitude."

11. In accordance with this paragraph, the proper attitude for a police officer to take is
   (A) to be pleasant and sympathetic at all times
   (C) to be stern and severe in meting out justice
   (B) to be friendly, firm and impartial to all
   (D) to avoid being rude, except in those cases where the public is uncooperative.

12. Assume that an officer is assigned by a superior officer to a busy highway intersection and is warned to be on the lookout for motorists who seem to be out of control or who are speeding or driving recklessly. According to this paragraph, it would be proper for the officer in this assignment to
   (A) give a summons to every motorist whose car momentarily crossed the center line
   (B) hide behind a truck and wait for drivers who violate traffic laws
   (C) select at random motorists who seem to be impatient and lecture them sternly on traffic safety
   (D) stand on post in order to deter violations and give offenders a summons or a warning as required.

13. According to this paragraph, a police officer must realize that the primary purpose of police work is to
   (A) provide proper police service in a courteous manner
   (B) decide whether those who violate the law should be punished
   (C) arrest those who violate laws
   (D) establish a proper employer-employee relationship.

Answer questions 14 to 17 solely on the basis of the following paragraph:

"When a vehicle has been disabled in the tunnel, the officer on patrol in this zone shall press the *emergency truck* light button. In the fast lane, red lights will go on throughout the tunnel; in the slow lane, amber lights will go on throughout the tunnel. The yellow zone light will go on at each signal control station throughout the tunnel and will flash the number of the zone in which the stoppage has occurred. A red flashing pilot light will appear only at the signal control station at which the *emergency truck* button was pressed. The emergency garage will receive an audible and visual signal indicating the signal control station at which the *emergency truck* button was pressed. The garage officer shall acknowledge receipt of the signal by pressing the acknowledgement button. This will cause the pilot light at the operated signal control station in the tunnel to cease flashing and to remain steady. It is an answer to the officer at the operated signal control station that the emergency truck is responding to the call."

14. According to this paragraph, when the *emergency truck* light button is pressed
   (A) amber lights will go on in every lane throughout the tunnel
   (B) emergency signal lights will go on only in the lane in which the disabled vehicle happens to be
   (C) red lights will go on in the fast lane throughout the tunnel
   (D) pilot lights at all signal control stations will turn amber.

15. According to this paragraph, the number of the zone in which the stoppage has occurred is flashed
   (A) immediately after all the lights in the tunnel turn red
   (B) by the yellow zone light at each signal control station
   (C) by the emergency truck at the point of stoppage
   (D) by the emergency garage.

16. According to this paragraph an officer near the disabled vehicle will know that the emergency tow truck is coming when
   (A) the pilot light at the operated signal control station appears and flashes red
   (B) an audible signal is heard in the tunnel
   (C) the zone light at the operated signal control station turns red
   (D) the pilot light at the operated signal control station becomes steady.

17. Under the system described in the above paragraph, it would be correct to come to the conclusion that
   (A) officers at all signal control stations are expected to acknowledge that they have received the stoppage signal
   (B) officers at all signal control stations will know where the stoppage has occurred
   (C) all traffic in both lanes of that side of the tunnel in which the stoppage has occurred must stop until the emergency truck has arrived
   (D) there are two emergency garages, each able to respond to stoppages in traffic going in one particular direction.

Answer questions 18 to 20 solely on the basis of the following quotation:

"In cases of accident it is most important for an officer to obtain the name, age, residence, occupation and a full description of the person injured, names and addresses of witnesses. The officer shall also obtain a statement of the attendant circumstances, and shall carefully note contributory conditions, if any, such as broken pavement, excavation, lights not burning, snow and ice on the roadway, etc. The officer shall enter all the facts in the memorandum book on Form NY-17 or Form NY-18, and promptly transmit the original form to a superior officer and the duplicate to headquarters.

An officer shall render reasonable assistance to sick or injured persons. If the circumstances appear to require the services of a physician, the officer shall summon a physician by telephoning the superior officer on duty and notifying the superior of the apparent nature of the illness or accident and location where the physician will be required. He or she may summon other officers to assist if circumstances warrant.

In case of an accident or where a person is sick on state property, an officer shall obtain the information necessary to fill out card form NY-18 and record this in the memorandum book and promptly telephone the facts to the superior officer. He or she shall deliver the original card at the expiration of the tour to the superior officer and transmit the duplicate to headquarters."

18. According to this quotation, the most important consideration in any report on a case of accident or injury is to
    (A) obtain all the facts
    (B) telephone the superior officer at once
    (C) obtain a statement of the attendant circumstances
    (D) determine ownership of the property on which the accident occurred.

19. According to this quotation, in the case of an accident on state property, the officer should always
    (A) summon a physician before filling out any forms or making any entries in the memorandum book
    (B) give the superior officer on duty a prompt report by telephone
    (C) immediately bring the original of Form NY-18 to the superior officer on duty
    (D) call at least one other officer to the scene to witness conditions.

20. If the procedures stated in this quotation were followed for all accidents in New York State, an impartial survey of accidents occurring during any period of time in this state may be most easily made by
    (A) asking a typical officer to show you the memorandum book
    (B) having a superior officer investigate whether contributory conditions mentioned by witnesses actually exist
    (C) checking all the records of all superior officers
    (D) checking the duplicate card files at headquarters.

Answer questions 21 and 22 on the basis of the following paragraph:

"The use of a roadblock is simply an adaptation to police practices of the military concept of encirclement. Successful operation of a roadblock plan depends almost entirely on the amount of advance study and planning given to such operations. A thorough and detailed examination of the roads and terrain under the jurisdiction of a given police agency should be made with the locations of the roadblocks pinpointed in advance. The first principle to be borne in mind in the location of each roadblock is the time element. Its location must be at a point beyond which the fugitive could not have possibly traveled in the time elapsed from the commission of the crime to the arrival of the officers at the roadblock."

21. According to this paragraph
    (A) military operations have made extensive use of roadblocks
    (B) the military concept of encirclement is an adaptation of police use of roadblocks
    (C) the technique of encirclement has been widely used by military forces
    (D) a roadblock is generally more effective than encirclement.

22. According to this paragraph
    (A) the factor of time is the sole consideration in the location of a roadblock
    (B) the maximum speed possible in the method of escape is of major importance in roadblock location
    (C) the time of arrival of officers at the site of a proposed roadblock is of little importance
    (D) if the method of escape is not known it should be assumed that the escape is by automobile.

Answer questions 23 to 25 on the basis of the following paragraph:

"A number of crimes, such as robbery, assault, rape, certain forms of theft and burglary, are high visibility crimes in that it is apparent to all concerned that they are criminal acts prior to or at the time they are committed. In contrast to these, check forgeries, especially those committed by first offenders, have low visibility. There is little in the criminal act or in the interaction between the check passer and the person cashing the check to identify it as a crime. Closely related to this special quality of the forgery crime is the fact that, while it is formally defined and treated as a felonious or 'infamous' crime, it is informally held by the legally untrained public to be a relatively harmless form of crime."

23. According to this paragraph, crimes of "high visibility"
    (A) are immediately recognized as crime by the victims
    (B) take place in public view
    (C) always involve violence or the threat of violence
    (D) usually are committed after dark.

24. According to this paragraph,
    (A) the public regards check forgery as a minor crime
    (B) the law regards check forgery as a minor crime
    (C) the law distinguishes between check forgery and other forgery
    (D) it is easier to spot inexperienced check forgers than other criminals.

25. As used in this paragraph, an "infamous" crime is
    (A) a crime attracting great attention from the public
    (B) more serious than a felony
    (C) less serious than a felony
    (D) more or less serious than a felony depending upon the surrounding circumstances.

Answer questions 26 and 27 on the basis of the following paragraph:

"The racketeer is primarily concerned with business affairs, legitimate or otherwise, and preferably those which are close to the margin of legitimacy. The racketeer gets the best opportunities from business organizations which meet the need of large sections of the public for goods or services which are defined as illegitimate by the same public, such as prostitution, gambling, illicit drugs or liquor.

In contrast to the thief, the racketeer and the establishments under control deliver goods and services for money received."

26. From this paragraph it can be deduced that suppression of racketeers is difficult because
    (A) victims of racketeers are not guilty of violating the law
    (B) racketeers are generally engaged in fully legitimate enterprises
    (C) many people want services which are not obtainable through legitimate sources
    (D) the racketeers are well organized.

27. According to this paragraph, racketeering, unlike theft, involves
    (A) objects of value
    (B) payment for goods received
    (C) organized gangs
    (D) public approval.

Answer questions 28 through 32 solely on the basis of the following paragraph:

"Lifting consists of transferring a print that has been dusted with powder to a transfer medium in order to preserve the print. Chemically developed prints cannot be lifted. Proper lifting of fingerprints is difficult and should be undertaken only when other means of recording the print are neither available nor suitable. Lifting should not be attempted from a porous surface. There are two types of commercial lifting tape which are good transfer mediums: rubber adhesive lift, one side of which is gummed and covered with thin, transparent celluloid; and transparent lifting tape, made of cellophane, one side of which is gummed. A package of acetate covers, frosted on one side and used to cover and protect the lifted print, accompanies each roll. If commercial tape is not available, transparent scotch tape may be used. The investigator should remove the celluloid or acetate cover from the lifting tape; smooth the tape, gummy side down, firmly and evenly over the entire print; gently peel the tape off the surface; replace the cover; and attach pertinent identifying data to the tape. All parts of the print should come in contact with the tape; air pockets should be avoided. The print will adhere to the lifting tape. The cover permits the print to be viewed and protects it from damage. Transparent lifting tape does not reverse the print. If a rubber adhesive lift is utilized, the print is reversed. Before a direct comparison can be made, the lifted print must be photographed, the negative reversed, and a positive made."

28. An investigator wishing to preserve a record of fingerprints on a highly porous surface should
    (A) develop them chemically before attempting to lift them
    (B) lift them with scotch tape only when no other means of recording the print are available
    (C) employ some method other than lifting
    (D) dust them with powder before attempting to lift them with rubber adhesive lift.

29. Disregarding all other considerations, the simplest process to use in *lifting a fingerprint* from a window pane is that involving the use of
    (A) rubber adhesive lift, because it gives a positive print in one step
    (B) dusting powder and a camera, because the photograph is less likely to break than the window pane
    (C) a chemical process, because it both develops and preserves the print at the same time
    (D) transparent lifting tape, because it does not reverse the print.

30. When a piece of commercial lifting tape is being used by an investigator wishing to lift a clear fingerprint from a smoothly-finished metal safe-door, he should
    (A) prevent the ends of the tape from getting stuck to the metal surface because of the danger of forming air-pockets and thus damaging the print
    (B) make certain that the tape covers all parts of the print and no air-pockets are formed
    (C) carefully roll the tape over the most significant parts of the print only to avoid forming air-pockets
    (D) be especially cautious not to destroy the air-pockets since this would tend to blur the print.

31. When fingerprints lifted from an object found at the scene of a crime are to be compared with the fingerprints of a suspect, the lifted print
    (A) can be compared directly only if a rubber adhesive lift was used
    (B) cannot be compared directly if transparent scotch tape was used
    (C) can be compared directly if transparent scotch tape was used
    (D) must be photographed first and a positive made if any commercial lifting tape was used.

32. When a rubber adhesive lift is to be used to lift a fingerprint, the one of the following which must be gently peeled off first is the
    (A) acetate cover
    (B) celluloid strip
    (C) dusted surface
    (D) tape off the print surface.

33. "In examining the scene of a homicide one should not only look for the usual, standard traces — fingerprints, footprints, etc. — but should also have eyes open for details which at first glance may not seem to have any connection with the crime." The most logical inference to be drawn from this statement is that
    (A) in general, standard traces are not important
    (B) sometimes one should not look for footprints
    (C) usually only the usual, standard traces are important
    (D) one cannot tell in advance what will be important.

34. "Pistols with the same number of barrel grooves may be differentiated by the direction of the twist of the rifling, which may be either to the left or to the right." Of the following statements, the one which can most accurately be inferred from the quotation is that
    (A) most pistols have the same number of grooves
    (B) some pistols have rifling twisted both left and right
    (C) the direction of the twist in any pistol can be either left or right
    (D) pistols with different numbers of grooves are rifled differently.

Answer questions 35 to 41 on the basis of the information appearing in the following paragraph:

"The first consideration in shooting a revolver is how to stand in a steady position. You may almost face the target in assuming a comfortable shooting stance, or you may face away from the target as much as ninety degrees, and still find it possible to stand easily and quietly. The principal point to observe is to spread the feet apart at least eight inches. This varies with the individual according to the length of his legs. Stand firmly on both feet. Do not bend either leg at the knee and be careful to develop a stance which does not allow the body to lean backward or forward. Ease and naturalness in posture with body muscles relaxed is the secret of good shooting form. The shooting arm should be straight, with the weight of the pistol supported not so much by the arm as by the muscles of the shoulder. Do not tense any muscle of the arm or hand while holding the revolver; especially avoid locking the elbow. The grip of the gun should be seated in the hand so that an imaginary line drawn along the forearm would pass through the bore of the gun. The heel of the hand should reach around the stock far enough to go past the center line of the gun. The thumb can be either alongside the hammer, on top of the frame, or it can be pointed downward toward the tip of the trigger finger. The high position is preferable, because when you are shooting rapid fire the thumb will have a shorter distance to move to reach the hammer spur."

35. The one of the following subjects discussed in this paragraph is the proper method of
(A) leading a moving target
(B) squeezing the trigger
(C) gripping the revolver
(D) using revolver sights.

36. According to this paragraph, the secret of good shooting form is
(A) proper sighting of the target
(B) a relaxed and natural position
(C) firing slowly and carefully
(D) keeping the thumb alongside the hammer.

37. For proper shooting stance, it is recommended that the weight of the pistol be supported by
(A) the muscles of the shoulder
(B) locking the elbow
(C) the muscles of the forearm
(D) tensing the wrist muscles.

38. The chief advantage of employing a high thumb position in firing a revolver is to
(A) maintain a more uniform grip
(B) achieve greater accuracy
(C) achieve better recoil control
(D) facilitate more rapid shooting.

39. When firing a revolver at a target, the angle at which you should face the target
(A) is 45 degrees
(B) is 90 degrees

(C) is greater for taller persons
(D) varies naturally from person to person.

40. According to this paragraph, the revolver should be held in such a manner that the
(A) bore of the revolver is slightly below the heel of the hand
(B) revolver, horizontally, is level with the shoulder
(C) center line of the revolver is a continuation of the forearm
(D) revolver is at a 45 degree angle with the target.

41. Of the following, the most accurate statement concerning proper shooting position is that the
(A) left knee should be bent slightly
(B) feet should be spread at least eight inches apart
(C) you should lean slightly forward as you fire each shot
(D) weight of the body should be on the right foot.

The paragraph below is selected from a typical uniformed force manual. Read the paragraph carefully and then answer questions 42 to 47 solely on the basis of the information appearing in the paragraph.

"The revolvers issued by this Department are of two makes: the .38 Colt Official Police and the .38 Smith and Wesson Special. The same ammunition, .38 Colt Special or .38 Smith and Wesson Special, is used in both guns. The principal difference between these revolvers is that the cylinder-releasing bolt knob on the Colt revolver is moved to the rear to release the cylinder releasing bolt, while on the Smith and Wesson this knob is moved to the front. The Colt can be cocked with the cylinder open, while with the Smith and Wesson the cylinder releasing bolt knob must be moved to the rear in order to do this. The Colt is heavier; 2 lbs. 1 oz. unloaded, 2 lbs. 4 oz. loaded; while the Smith and Wesson weighs 1 lb. 14 oz. unloaded and 2 lbs. 1 oz. loaded. These revolvers are unquestionably among the best made. No other revolver, with the possible exception of the English Wembly, approaches their quality. The muzzle velocity of these revolvers, using standard ammunition, is 879 feet per second. The chamber pressure is 12,000 lbs. per square inch. The fixed sights are set for approximately 25 yards."

42. On the basis of this paragraph, the revolvers which have the same weight are the
(A) Smith and Wesson, loaded, and the Colt,

loaded

(B) Colt, unloaded, and the Smith and Wesson unloaded

(C) Smith and Wesson, loaded, and the Colt, unloaded

(D) Colt, loaded, and the Smith and Wesson, unloaded.

43. Of the following, the most accurate statement of a difference between the .38 Colt Official Police and the .38 Smith and Wesson Special is that the Colt, unlike the Smith and Wesson,
(A) has a muzzle velocity of 879 feet
(B) has a cylinder-releasing bolt
(C) uses .38 Smith and Wesson ammunition
(D) can be cocked with the cylinder open.

44. Of the following, the most accurate statement that can be made concerning the English Wembly, solely on the basis of the preceding paragraph is that it
(A) weighs more than 2 lbs. unloaded
(B) compares favorably with the best revolvers made
(C) uses .38 Colt or Smith and Wesson ammunition
(D) has a chamber pressure exceeding 12,000 lbs. per square inch.

45. In the above paragraph, the number .38 refers most accurately to the
(A) diameter of the bore
(B) length of the bullet
(C) circumference of the cartridge
(D) thickness of the cylinder.

46. As used in the preceding paragraph, the term muzzle refers most accurately to the
(A) acceleration of the projectile in flight
(B) average speed of the bullet in flight
(C) rate of expansion of the gases in the muzzle
(D) speed at which the bullet leaves the revolver.

47. Of the following, the least accurate statement concerning the two revolvers issued by the Department, on the basis of the preceding paragraph, is that both
(A) can use the same ammunition
(B) have a cylinder-releasing bolt knob
(C) have adjustable sights
(D) have a chamber pressure of 12,000 lbs. per square inch.

ANSWER KEY

1. D	9. C	17. B	25. C	33. D	41. B
2. A	10. B	18. A	26. C	34. C	42. C
3. D	11. B	19. B	27. B	35. C	43. D
4. B	12. D	20. D	28. C	36. B	44. B
5. A	13. A	21. C	29. D	37. A	45. A
6. C	14. C	22. B	30. B	38. D	46. D
7. C	15. B	23. A	31. C	39. D	47. C
8. A	16. D	24. A	32. B	40. C	

ANSWER SHEET FOR READING QUESTIONS ON STATE LAW

TEST I. STATE PENAL LAW

1 Ⓐ Ⓑ Ⓒ Ⓓ	6 Ⓐ Ⓑ Ⓒ Ⓓ	11 Ⓐ Ⓑ Ⓒ Ⓓ	16 Ⓐ Ⓑ Ⓒ Ⓓ
2 Ⓐ Ⓑ Ⓒ Ⓓ	7 Ⓐ Ⓑ Ⓒ Ⓓ	12 Ⓐ Ⓑ Ⓒ Ⓓ	17 Ⓐ Ⓑ Ⓒ Ⓓ
3 Ⓐ Ⓑ Ⓒ Ⓓ	8 Ⓐ Ⓑ Ⓒ Ⓓ	13 Ⓐ Ⓑ Ⓒ Ⓓ	18 Ⓐ Ⓑ Ⓒ Ⓓ
4 Ⓐ Ⓑ Ⓒ Ⓓ	9 Ⓐ Ⓑ Ⓒ Ⓓ	14 Ⓐ Ⓑ Ⓒ Ⓓ	19 Ⓐ Ⓑ Ⓒ Ⓓ
5 Ⓐ Ⓑ Ⓒ Ⓓ	10 Ⓐ Ⓑ Ⓒ Ⓓ	15 Ⓐ Ⓑ Ⓒ Ⓓ	20 Ⓐ Ⓑ Ⓒ Ⓓ

TEST II. STATE CORRECTION LAW

1 Ⓐ Ⓑ Ⓒ Ⓓ	7 Ⓐ Ⓑ Ⓒ Ⓓ	13 Ⓐ Ⓑ Ⓒ Ⓓ	19 Ⓐ Ⓑ Ⓒ Ⓓ	25 Ⓐ Ⓑ Ⓒ Ⓓ
2 Ⓐ Ⓑ Ⓒ Ⓓ	8 Ⓐ Ⓑ Ⓒ Ⓓ	14 Ⓐ Ⓑ Ⓒ Ⓓ	20 Ⓐ Ⓑ Ⓒ Ⓓ	26 Ⓐ Ⓑ Ⓒ Ⓓ
3 Ⓐ Ⓑ Ⓒ Ⓓ	9 Ⓐ Ⓑ Ⓒ Ⓓ	15 Ⓐ Ⓑ Ⓒ Ⓓ	21 Ⓐ Ⓑ Ⓒ Ⓓ	27 Ⓐ Ⓑ Ⓒ Ⓓ
4 Ⓐ Ⓑ Ⓒ Ⓓ	10 Ⓐ Ⓑ Ⓒ Ⓓ	16 Ⓐ Ⓑ Ⓒ Ⓓ	22 Ⓐ Ⓑ Ⓒ Ⓓ	28 Ⓐ Ⓑ Ⓒ Ⓓ
5 Ⓐ Ⓑ Ⓒ Ⓓ	11 Ⓐ Ⓑ Ⓒ Ⓓ	17 Ⓐ Ⓑ Ⓒ Ⓓ	23 Ⓐ Ⓑ Ⓒ Ⓓ	29 Ⓐ Ⓑ Ⓒ Ⓓ
6 Ⓐ Ⓑ Ⓒ Ⓓ	12 Ⓐ Ⓑ Ⓒ Ⓓ	18 Ⓐ Ⓑ Ⓒ Ⓓ	24 Ⓐ Ⓑ Ⓒ Ⓓ	30 Ⓐ Ⓑ Ⓒ Ⓓ

TEST III. STATE CORRECTION LAW

1 Ⓐ Ⓑ Ⓒ Ⓓ	7 Ⓐ Ⓑ Ⓒ Ⓓ	13 Ⓐ Ⓑ Ⓒ Ⓓ	19 Ⓐ Ⓑ Ⓒ Ⓓ	25 Ⓐ Ⓑ Ⓒ Ⓓ
2 Ⓐ Ⓑ Ⓒ Ⓓ	8 Ⓐ Ⓑ Ⓒ Ⓓ	14 Ⓐ Ⓑ Ⓒ Ⓓ	20 Ⓐ Ⓑ Ⓒ Ⓓ	26 Ⓐ Ⓑ Ⓒ Ⓓ
3 Ⓐ Ⓑ Ⓒ Ⓓ	9 Ⓐ Ⓑ Ⓒ Ⓓ	15 Ⓐ Ⓑ Ⓒ Ⓓ	21 Ⓐ Ⓑ Ⓒ Ⓓ	27 Ⓐ Ⓑ Ⓒ Ⓓ
4 Ⓐ Ⓑ Ⓒ Ⓓ	10 Ⓐ Ⓑ Ⓒ Ⓓ	16 Ⓐ Ⓑ Ⓒ Ⓓ	22 Ⓐ Ⓑ Ⓒ Ⓓ	28 Ⓐ Ⓑ Ⓒ Ⓓ
5 Ⓐ Ⓑ Ⓒ Ⓓ	11 Ⓐ Ⓑ Ⓒ Ⓓ	17 Ⓐ Ⓑ Ⓒ Ⓓ	23 Ⓐ Ⓑ Ⓒ Ⓓ	29 Ⓐ Ⓑ Ⓒ Ⓓ
6 Ⓐ Ⓑ Ⓒ Ⓓ	12 Ⓐ Ⓑ Ⓒ Ⓓ	18 Ⓐ Ⓑ Ⓒ Ⓓ	24 Ⓐ Ⓑ Ⓒ Ⓓ	30 Ⓐ Ⓑ Ⓒ Ⓓ

READING QUESTIONS ON STATE LAW

TEST I. STATE PENAL LAW

TIME: 25 Minutes.

DIRECTIONS: *This test consists of several reading passages, each followed by a number of statements. Analyze each statement solely on the basis of the material given. Then, mark your answer sheet*
(A) *if the statement is entirely true.*
(B) *if the statement is entirely false.*
(C) *if the statement is partially false and partially true.*
(D) *if the statement cannot be judged on the basis of the facts given in the excerpt.*

The answer key for this test appears at the end of the section.

READING PASSAGE

"A crime is an act or omission forbidden by law, and punishable upon conviction by death; or imprisonment; or fine; or removal from office; or disqualification to hold any office of trust, honor or profit under the state; or other penal discipline. Except that the acts defined as traffic infractions by the vehicle and traffic law, heretofore or hereafter committed, are not crimes. A crime is either a felony or a misdemeanor. A felony is a crime which may be punishable by death; or imprisonment in a state prison. A misdemeanor is any other crime."

1. A public official convicted of a crime is no longer eligible to hold public office.

2. A traffic infraction is sometimes a felony or else a misdemeanor.

3. A crime is generally defined as an act or omission under the law.

4. A misdemeanor is a crime, which may be punished by imprisonment in a state prison.

5. A crime is most often punished by imprisonment.

READING PASSAGE

"A person concerned in the commission of a crime, whether he or she directly commits the act of constituting the offense or aids and abets in its commission, and whether present or absent, and a person who directly or indirectly counsels, commands, induces or procures another to commit a crime is a 'principal.' A person who, after the commission of a felony, harbors, conceals, or aids the offender, with the intent that he or she may avoid or escape from arrest, trial, conviction, or punishment, having knowledge or reasonable ground to believe that such offender is liable to arrest, has been arrested, is indicted or convicted, or has committed a felony, is an 'accessory' to the felony."

6. Harboring a criminal after commission of a crime is a criminal offense.

7. A 'principal' in the commission of a crime is liable to more severe punishment than an 'accessory.'

8. A person who indirectly induces another to refuse to commit a crime is generally termed an 'accessory.'

9. The action of an 'accessory' to a felony generally is one occurring when the crime has already been perpetrated, whereas the action of a 'principal' always occurs before the crime is committed.

10. Abetting another in the commission of a crime is an action, the perpetrator of which is legally termed a 'principal.'

READING PASSAGE

"A person, who, not being authorized by law, visits any state prison, reformatory, penitentiary, or other place for the detention of persons convicted of crime or who communicates with any prisoner therein without the consent of the agent or warden, superintendent, keeper, or other person having charge thereof; or, without such consent, brings into or conveys out of a state prison, reformatory, penitentiary or other place for the detention of persons convicted of crime, any letter, information or writing to or from any prisoner, is guilty of a misdemeanor."

11. A state prisoner is not generally permitted to receive personal letters.

12. A person, who, after visiting a state prison, leaves with a letter from the prisoner to his or her family, must be considered guilty of a misdemeanor.

13. An unauthorized person may not communicate with a person imprisoned in a state prison.

14. No state prisoner may receive a communication legally without the approval of a prison officer.

15. A person visiting a state prisoner and not having the keeper's written permission is guilty of a misdemeanor.

READING PASSAGE

"Any person who conveys into or takes from any state prison, reformatory or penitentiary, or other place for the detention of persons convicted of crime, or who personally or through any other person or persons gives, sells, furnishes or otherwise delivers to any prisoner, or prisoners in custody, any drug, liquor or any article prohibited by law or by the rules of the superintendent, keeper or other official having charge or control thereof, is guilty of a misdemeanor."

16. Only articles prohibited by law are denied a state prisoner.

17. A person delivering a state prisoner a drug prohibited by law, with the consent of the keeper, is not guilty of a misdemeanor.

18. Under no circumstances is a state prisoner permitted to drink intoxicating liquors.

19. Although a drug may not be legally delivered to a prisoner by an outside person, the opposite is true in the case of certain liquors.

20. A prison guard furnishing an unauthorized drug to a prisoner is guilty of a misdemeanor.

State Trooper

TEST II. STATE CORRECTION LAW

TIME: 30 Minutes.

DIRECTIONS: *This test consists of several reading passages, each followed by a number of statements. Analyze each statement solely on the basis of the material given. Then, mark your answer sheet*
  (A) *if the statement is entirely true.*
  (B) *if the statement is entirely false.*
  (C) *if the statement is partially false and partially true.*
  (D) *if the statement cannot be judged on the basis of the facts given in the excerpt.*

The answer key for this test appears at the end of the section.

READING PASSAGE

"The objective of prison education, in its broadest sense, should be the socialization of the inmates through varied impressional and expressional activities, with emphasis on individual inmate needs. The objective of this program shall be the return of these inmates to society with a more wholesome attitude toward living, with a desire to conduct themselves as good citizens, and with the skill and knowledge which will give them a reasonable chance to maintain themselves and their dependents through honest labor. To this end, each prisoner shall be given a program of education, which, on the basis of available data, seems most likely to further the process of socialization and rehabilitation."

1. Machine shop work is a good example of an expressional activity.

2. The educational program advocated for prisoners is designed for their rehabilitation, but not their socialization.

3. Group needs, as distinguished from individual needs, should be given the greater consideration in the socialization of prison inmates.

4. A confirmed criminal can rarely be induced to become a good citizen.

5. The socialization process includes the acquisition of skills and knowledge on the part of prison inmates.

READING PASSAGE

"No officer or employee in any prison shall inflict any blows whatever upon any prisoner, except in self-defense, or to suppress a revolt or insurrection. When several prisoners combine, or any single prisoner shall offer violence to any officer of a state prison, or to any other prisoner, or do or attempt to do any injury to the building or any workshop, or any property therein, or shall attempt to escape, or shall resist or disobey any lawful command, the officers of the prison shall use all suitable means to defend themselves, to enforce observation of discipline, to secure the persons of the offenders, and to prevent any such attempt or escape."

6. A prison officer may go to any suitable extreme in preventing prison breaks.

7. If a prisoner is escaping, he or she should be ordered to halt before being fired upon.

8. A prison guard by strike a prisoner only if the latter provokes the guard verbally.

9. The duties of prison officers include the enforcement of discipline on the part of inmates, but under no circumstances may a prison officer strike a prisoner in the enforcement of such discipline.

10. Self-defense is the only legitimate excuse for physically inflicting injury upon a prison inmate.

READING PASSAGE

"Whenever any prisoner confined in a state prison, and not released on parole, shall escape therefrom, it shall be the duty of the warden to take all proper measures for the apprehension of the prisoner so escaped; and in his or her discretion may offer a reward not exceeding fifty dollars for the apprehension and delivery of every such escaped prisoner. Any such prisoner, escaped from any state prison in this state, and afterwards arrested, shall serve out the full balance of the sentence remaining unexpired at the time of such escape. All rewards and other sums of money paid for so advertising and apprehending any such escaped prisoner shall be paid by the warden out of the funds of the prison."

11. An escaped prisoner, upon being apprehended, must serve a year in prison if this is the amount of the full balance of the sentence remaining unexpired at the time of the escape.

12. An apprehended prisoner, returned to a state prison after having escaped, must serve the entire sentence again.

13. State prisoners are generally released on parole.

14. Reward money for an escaped prisoner's apprehension is generally paid out of the warden's funds.

15. The warden is most concerned with the apprehension of an escaped prisoner and may offer an unlimited reward for the delivery of this prisoner.

READING PASSAGE

"The Commissioner of Correction may make rules and regulations for the promotion or reduction of the prisoners from one classification to another, and shall transfer from time to time the prisoners in the state prisons from one prison to another with reference to the respective capacities of the several state prisons, or with reference to the health or reformation of the prisoners, or with reference to including all prisoners of one classification as nearly as may be practical in one prison, or, may direct the separation from each other of the prisoners of different classifications so far as practicable within each state prison."

16. Health conditions sometimes necessitate the transfer of prisoners from one state prison to another.

17. Prisoners are classified as to the nature of their crime and are kept in those prisons which correspond exactly to their particular classification.

18. A state prisoner may be promoted or demoted from one classification to another in accordance with the rules and regulations set forth by the Commissioner of Correction.

19. Prisoners are sometimes transferred from one prison to another by the Commissioner of Correction, the chief purpose of the transfer being the bringing together of prisoners of dissimilar classification.

20. It is the duty of the prison guard to effect the transfer of prisoners from one prison to another.

READING PASSAGE

"Whenever there shall be a sufficient number of cells in the prison, it shall be the duty of the warden to keep each prisoner single in the cell at night, and also in the daytime when the prisoner is not employed, or in a hospital, or engaged in other duties or recreation in accordance with the rules of the Department of Correction. The clothing and bedding of the prisoners shall be manufactured as far as practicable in the prison. The prisoners shall be supplied with a sufficient quantity of wholesome food."

21. Prison rules require that prisoners' food be adequate as well as healthful.

22. All prisoners' clothing is manufactured by the prisoners themselves.

23. Under no circumstances are more than two prisoners kept in a prison cell.

24. No prison bedding is ever manufactured outside of the prison.

25. No more than one unemployed prisoner is generally kept in a cell during the daytime.

READING PASSAGE

"If, in the opinion of the warden of a state prison, it shall be deemed necessary to inflict unusual punishment in order to produce the entire submission or obedience of any prisoner, it shall be the duty of such warden to confine each prisoner immediately in a cell, upon a short allowance, and to retain the prisoner therein until reduced to submission and obedience. The short allowance of each prisoner shall be prescribed by the physician, whose duty it shall be to visit such prisoner and examine daily into the state of his or her health until the prisoner be released from solitary confinement and returned to labor."

26. **Solitary confinement is prescribed only when a prisoner is disobedient or will not submit to orders.**

27. A prisoner ordered to solitary confinement may not be released until reduced to submission and obedience.

28. It falls within the duties of the warden to put a prisoner upon a short allowance and to prescribe its nature.

29. **A prisoner on short allowance does not necessarily need a physician's attention.**

30. Solitary confinement and a short allowance is not considered unusual punishment.

TEST III. STATE CORRECTION LAW

TIME: 30 Minutes.

DIRECTIONS: This test consists of several reading passages, each followed by a number of statements. Analyze each statement solely on the basis of the material given. Then, mark your answer sheet (A) (B) (C) or (D).
Mark it (A) if the statement is entirely true.
Mark it (B) if the statement is entirely false.
Mark it (C) if the statement is partially false and partially true.
Mark it (D) if the statement cannot be judged on the basis of the facts given in the excerpt.

The answer key for this test appears at the end of the section.

READING PASSAGE

"In case any pestilence or contagious disease shall break out among the prisoners of any of the state prisons, or in the vicinity of such prisons, the Commissioner of Correction may cause the prisoners confined to such prison, or any of them, to be removed to some suitable place of security, where such of them as may be sick shall receive all necessary care and medical assistance; such prisoners shall be returned as soon as may be to the state prison from which they were taken, to be confined therein according to their respective sentences."

1. Medical assistance must necessarily be provided a sick patient removed from a prison to a place of security.

2. An epidemic raging in a nearby town may necessitate the removal of all inmates of a state prison to a place of security, but their return is imperative upon the cessation of the epidemic.

3. When a contagious disease breaks out among the prisoners of a state prison, only the sick may be ordered removed.

4. If the illness of a patient necessitates removal to a hospital for the period of six months, this period constitutes part of his or her sentence served and need not be served again.

5. A prisoner recovered from a contagious disease, having been removed to a hospital during the course of illness, has the option of remaining there to complete the sentence.

READING PASSAGE

"The Commissioner of Correction and the superintendents of all penitentiaries in the state, shall, so far as practicable, cause all the prisoners in the state correctional institutions and such penitentiaries, who are physically capable thereof, to be employed at hard labor, not to exceed eight hours of each day, other than Sundays and public holidays, but such hard labor shall be either for the purpose of production of supplies for said institutions or for the state or any political division thereof, or for any public institution owned or managed and controlled by the state; or for the purpose of industrial training, or partly for one, and partly for the other of such purposes."

6. State convict labor may be used to supply products for any institution controlled by the state.

7. Supplies manufactured by prisoners in a state prison must be utilized within the said institution.

8. A prisoner in good physical condition may generally be employed beyond eight hours at hard labor in a state prison.

9. The chief aim in forcing prison inmates to work is to provide them with industrial training.

10. Although state prisoners do not work on Sundays, they generally must put in a half day on public holidays.

READING PASSAGE

"The Commissioner of Correction may employ or cause to be employed the prisoners confined in the state prisons, in the repair, maintenance, construction or improvement of the public highways at any place within the state, outside of an incorporated village or city, upon request or with the consent of the superintendent of public works, in the case of state or county highways. When engaged in the maintenance and repair of a highway under the jurisdiction of county or town authorities, the county or town receiving the benefit of such labor shall pay such reasonable compensation as may be agreed upon, not exceeding one dollar per day for each prisoner."

11. A public highway within a city may not be constructed by state prison labor.

12. When a highway under the jurisdiction of a town is being repaired by state prison labor, such labor must be compensated for at the rate of more than one dollar per day for each prisoner.

13. State prisoners may be assigned to work on the public highways of the state, except that they may not be employed on public highways under the jurisdiction of a town or county.

14. State highways are generally maintained by prison labor.

15. Prison labor may be used on state highways only with the consent or upon the request of the superintendent of public works.

READING PASSAGE

"Any person interfering with or in any way interrupting the work of any prisoner employed upon the public highways, or any person giving or attempting to give any intoxicating liquors, beer, ale or other spirituous beverage to any prisoner so employed, shall be guilty of a misdemeanor. Any officer or employee of any state correctional institution having in charge the convicts employed upon such highways, may arrest without a warrant any person violating any above-mentioned provision."

16. Only non-toxicating liquors may be offered by a civilian to a prisoner working on a state highway.

17. Under no circumstances may a state prisoner be allowed intoxicating liquors or beer.

18. It is unlawful for a civilian to interfere with a prisoner working on a public highway.

19. A person offering any spirituous beverage to a state prisoner working on a highway may be arrested by the correction officer in charge, in the event the latter can provide a warrant.

20. A misdemeanor is not generally considered a serious offense.

READING PASSAGE

"The warden of a state prison shall take charge of all monies and other articles which may be brought to the prison by the convicts, and shall cause the same, immediately upon the receipt thereof, to be entered by the warden or the chief clerk among the receipts of the prison; which money and other articles, whenever the convict from whom the same was received, shall be discharged from prison, or the same shall be otherwise legally demanded, shall be returned by the said warden to such convict or other person legally entitled to the same, and vouchers shall be taken therefor."

21. A convict, upon entering a state prison, must relinquish all but personal articles.

22. A prisoner's money and other articles, taken upon entrance to a state prison, may be withheld from the prisoner and returned to some other person when legally demanded.

23. It is the duty of the chief clerk in a state prison to take charge of all monies brought into a prison by a convict, as well as to enter them among the receipts of the prison.

24. It is not necessary to make out a voucher for money returned from the prison receipts to a discharged prisoner.

25. As a rule, money taken from a convict is not returned upon discharge, unless legally demanded.

READING PASSAGE

"Whenever the transfer of prisoners from one state prison to another shall be ordered by the Commissioner of Correction, the warden of the prison from which such transfer is to be made, shall cause the prisoners to be sufficiently chained in pairs so far as practicable, and be transferred to the prison to which they are so ordered. The persons so employed to transport such prisoners shall prohibit all intercourse between them, and may inflict any reasonable and necessary correction upon such prisoners for disobedience or misconduct in any respect. In making such transfers, the Commissioner of Correction shall take into consideration the adaptability of the prisoners to the industries in the prisons to which they are transferred."

26. Motor vehicles are generally used to convey prisoners in groups from one prison to another.

27. A factor in the transfer of state prisoners from one institution to another is the nature of the type of industry in the prison.

28. Prisoners need not necessarily be chained in being transferred from one state prison to another.

29. A prison guard, employed in the transfer of prisoners from one to another state prison, may inflict any necessary punishment upon a prisoner for disobediency.

30. Prisoners being transferred from one state prison to another are not generally permitted to hold conversation among themselves.

ANSWER KEY TEST I

1.D	5.D	9.C	13.A	17.B
2.B	6.D	10.A	14.A	18.D
3.B	7.D	11.D	15.B	19.C
4.C	8.B	12.B	16.B	20.A

— ANSWER KEY TEST II

1.D	5.A	9.C	13.D	17.D	21.A	25.A	29.B
2.C	6.A	10.B	14.B	18.A	22.D	26.D	30.B
3.B	7.D	11.A	15.C	19.C	23.D	27.A	
4.D	8.B	12.B	16.A	20.B	24.B	28.C	

ANSWER KEY TEST III

1.A	5.B	9.D	13.C	17.D	21.B	25.B	29.A
2.A	6.A	10.C	14.D	18.A	22.A	26.D	30.A
3.B	7.B	11.A	15.A	19.C	23.C	27.A	
4.D	8.B	12.B	16.B	20.D	24.B	28.B	

MAKING REPORTS

In work like yours, reports would normally be required of you from time to time. Sometimes, it might be an informal, oral reply to a request for information. And then it might be a full written statement based upon a great amount of careful study. If your reports are on the beam, your reputation for dependability and sound staff work is enhanced. On the other hand, each request puts you on the spot. Since your test will undoubtedly seek to elicit your ability to make reports, you should take this opportunity to find out how to score high.

PURPOSE OF REPORTS

Before we get into the methods of making reports, it might be wise to clear our thinking as to the purpose behind them.

WHAT IS THE PRIMARY REASON FOR MAKING REPORTS

—They supply the information needed by officials above us
—They are necessary in order to maintain control of operations
—Top management must have full knowledge of what goes on in order to plan properly

WHY DO THEY COME TO US FOR THE FACTS? WHY DON'T THEY FIND OUT FOR THEMSELVES?

—We happen to be the best source of information about the work
—We are closest to operations and know the most about working conditions
—Our point of view may be more practical and realistic than that of people farther removed from operations
—It is our responsibility as part of the management team to contribute to the smooth running of the installation

NATURE OF REPORTING

The reports we are called upon to make from time to time are not all the same.

WHAT DIFFERENT KINDS OF REPORTS DO WE DEAL WITH?

It is only natural that the nature of reports should differ. Any work situation—shop, office, or field—is highly complicated. Equipment breaks down, people get sick or go fishing, and accidents will occur. We never know when these things are going to happen; yet management must be prepared—must be able to plan intelligently—must try to predict the unpredictable.

TYPES OF REPORTS	
By Content	By Time
—Production data	—Periodic
—Time reports	Daily
—Cost records	Weekly
—Explanation requested	Monthly
—Reasons asked for	—Special
—Recommendation	When necessary
—Suggestions	When called for

S1335

WHO, THEN, GETS THE REPORTS WE MAKE?

1. **Line**

   —Our chief, mainly
   —Division chief
   - -Commanding officer
   —Headquarters offices
   —Departmental offices

2. **Staff**

   —Management office
   —Safety office

   —Personnel office
   —Medical office

3. **Committees, Such As—**

   —Promotion
   —Deferment
   —Career development
   —Board of examiners

There may be other places that ask us for information from time to time. Many such requests are infrequent, on special matters that require a one-time answer. Others may be regular scheduled reports that constitute a continuous flow of essential information upward.

GETTING READY TO REPORT

So much for the general nature of reports. Now let us think about what we do to get ready to make a report, whether it is oral or written, special or periodic.

It may be desirable at this point to work with a specific example—an actual report that one of the supervisors has to make. There may be a periodic report with which several persons are familiar.

PREPARATIONS

—Defining the Subject
    —for clarity and understanding
    —to set limits to it
    —to meet the needs of the recipient

—Gathering the facts
    —data from records
    —observed facts
    —opinions and expressions

—Organizing the Facts
    —sifting out the unimportant
    —putting in logical order
    —striving for "punch," climax
    —conclusions and recommendations

KNOWING EXACTLY WHAT IS WANTED

What is the first thing we have to be sure about when we start to work on a report?

—Checking the instructions
—Being sure we understand

—Asking for explanation of points not clear
—Setting the limits; only what is wanted
—Finding out who will use the report
—Planning to meet the needs of those who will use it

GETTING THE FACTS TOGETHER

How do we go about getting the information we need?

—Deciding on the kind of information needed
—Using data already available in records
—Getting new facts that are pertinent
—Asking questions of our employees who may help
—Probing opinions to find out why people have that impression
—Putting the items down on paper so they will not be lost

ORGANIZING THE FACTS

What do we do with the facts after we get them?

—Bring together those that are related as to time, place, persons, cause, and effect
—Discard irrelevant facts
—Arrange them in a smooth order
—Check for breaks in continuity; rough spots
—Be sure they make sense
—Build up to an effective climax
—When desired, state your conclusions and recommendations based upon the facts

MAKING AN ORAL REPORT

Probably the most common method of reporting is by word of mouth. Many times we are asked questions such as—

—"What is the situation in the maintenance shop?"

—"What do you know about the delay in clearing X-52 requisitions?"

—"Will you find out whether your people are using too much sick leave?"

—"Can we ship out that bulldozer by 3 o'clock tomorrow?"

In each of these cases, somebody wants a report and usually we don't bother to write it out; we give an oral report.

ANSWERING WITHOUT OPPORTUNITY TO STUDY THE SITUATION

What do we do when the chief wants an answer to his question, "Right Now?"

—There is little time to prepare our reply

—Usually we can pause for a moment to get our thoughts in order

—We recall what we know about the situation—the facts

—We quickly organize our information so that it makes sense as we tell it

—If we are wise, we will protect ourselves by some expression such as—

—"This is the condition as I understand it now"

—"Without a complete check, it would appear * * *"

—"As I see it at this time * * *"

—"This is a tentative opinion—I shall check with the shop to confirm it"

ORAL REPORTING AFTER PREPARATION

If we have some opportunity to get ready to tell our story, how can we make our presentation effective?

It may be desirable to discuss briefly those borderline cases where speed in getting the answer back to management is important. The group should not have difficulty in agreeing that in these instances we drop other things, obtain only key facts essential to make a quick decision, and report promptly.

Effective Oral Reporting

—Know what you are going to say

—Have brief outline or notes

—If "showing" will help, have the material ready (charts, parts, etc.)

—Be alert

—Speak clearly

—Stop as soon as you are finished

An effective public speaker once said that when he appeared before an audience he tried to remember three things—

—To stand up so they would see him

—To speak up so they could hear him

—To shut up so they would like him

This is sound advice, even when our audience is limited to one person.

WRITING A REPORT

For many of us, it is a difficult task to prepare a written report. Of course, if it is merely filling in figures on a form, usually there is not much of a problem. But when we have to *write it out,* for higher officials to read, we are not so happy. We are not different from most people in this respect. It is not easy to express one's self in writing. Let us see if we can pool our ideas on how to do this effectively.

Highlights in Report Writing

—Always use an outline

—Keep on the beam—to the point

—Be concise

—Get someone else to read and criticize it

—Put lengthy explanations in attachments

—Make enough copies

USE OF OUTLINE

Why do we spend time making an outline if we know what we want to say?

—It helps to get material in the right order
—It aids our thinking through of the report as a whole
—It enables us to be sure that all important points are included, and that unimportant details are left out
—Changes can be made in an outline more easily than in a completed draft

WRITING DIRECTLY ON THE SUBJECT

What difference does it make if some irrelevant matters are included?

—Makes it more difficult for the reader to follow
—Wastes valuable time of the reader
—Gives him a poor impression of our ability to think clearly

ELIMINATING USELESS WORDS AND PHRASES

Why is conciseness so important?

—Saves time of writer, typist, and reader
—Makes the report much more forceful
—Takes the "hot air" out of it

GETTING A CRITICAL REVIEW

Why does it help to have someone else criticize the draft of the report?

—Finds parts that are not clear
—Recognizes "rough spots," where flow of thought is not smooth
—Assists in reducing wordiness

USE OF ATTACHMENTS

What are the advantages of using tabs and attachments on a report?

—Permits the report itself to be shorter, more readable, and more forceful
—Enables the reader to refer to supporting data or illustrative materials if desired
—Permits the reader to find quickly the exact items desired
—Supports the body of the report with factual data
—Adds to the strength without adding to the length

SUFFICIENT COPIES

Why do we want more than one copy?

—So the person receiving the report can refer to other interested parties
—Several people may want to use it at the same time
—If the report is important enough to prepare, copies should go in the files

IMPROVING OUR REPORTING

The quality of the reports we make to officials higher up in the organization has a great deal to do with our reputation as good managers. It would appear worthwhile, therefore, to spend a little time to see how we can improve our reporting. We already have brought out some valuable hints in our discussions of getting ready and actually making the reports. There are two or three questions we might well ask ourselves to check up on the effectiveness of our reporting.

IS THIS REPORT NECESSARY?

Why should we ask this question?

—Sometimes a report continues to be made after its usefulness is past
—The same data may be available from another source
—Maybe it is just filed—no one uses it
—A tactful question as to how it is used will show your chief that you are alert and interested

IS THIS REPORT ADEQUATE?

Why is this question significant?

—It forces us to put ourselves in the position of the one who is to get it
—It will bring out whether the report is usable
—It may lead to corrections or changes that increase its effectiveness
—It makes us review the report in terms of its purpose

IS THIS REPORT TIMELY?

Why is timeliness important?

—Important decisions at higher level may be held up

—There may be heavy pressure on our chief for an answer

—A report that is too late has lost its usefulness

MECHANICAL MAKE-UP OF A REPORT

We divide the subject of reports into two categories. We have the long report and the short report. It is as simple as that. The requirements of each of these types are somewhat different. The long report is one that usually consists of a half dozen or more pages. It is usually bound. It contains a letter of transmittal, a formal introduction, a discussion of the facts, a resume, conclusions, and recommendations. The short report may be set up in one of two ways. First, it may be set up as a letter, containing the same mechanical make-up as the letter. That is, you have the date on top, the inside address, and the salutation. You may begin your report "In accordance with your request, I am submitting . . . ," indicating the subject of your report, and you continue with whatever facts are desired in the report. You will have conclusions, if they are called for; and if recommendations are needed, those will be indicated too, at the end of the report. You conclude with the complimentary closing and your signature. Instead of closing with "Very truly yours," it is customary to write "Respectfully submitted."

The letter set-up is one form of the short or informal report. Again, you may set up the report in memorandum form. The form hasn't the usual letterhead, but it reads To, From, Subject. After To, you write the name of the person to whom you are sending the report; after From, you write your name; after Subject, you indicate the subject of the report. Then, without further introduction, you go right into the body of the report. What are the facts? What are your conclusions? What are your recommendations? There is usually no signature on such a report. Your name on the top gives authority for the statements in the report.

STYLE AND TONE OF REPORTS

In the long report, it is not customary to refer to yourself as I or we. You usually speak of the writer or the undersigned. You may, too, use some passive voice form like "Upon investigation it was learned that . . ." The reason you do not refer to yourself personally in the long report is that you want the report to sound very objective and scientific rather than subjective or personal. You want to give the impression that the material in the report consists of actual facts, unbiased facts, discovered through investigation, and that you are not injecting your personal views or prejudices. That is the reason why in the long report you do not make personal references to yourself. However, in the short report you may use those personal references. You may if you wish give an opinion if the opinion will be valued.

OPINION AND FACT

You have to be able to distinguish between a fact and an opinion if you are going to write a good report. After all, a report differs from a letter in that the report is more objective, more scientific. In a letter you may be very personal. In a report you can't afford to be because many important decisions may be based on the information in it. You are the investigator. You discover certain facts. It shouldn't be necessary for anyone to check on you, but it is desirable that your facts be facts, that is, that your information be accurate; and if you are going to have facts in your report you must know the difference between a fact and an opinion. A fact is a verifiable truth. In other words, it is something we can prove. An opinion, on the other hand, has no weight as evidence. It can't be proved. We shall deal in facts and opinions. In a report it is important that you state the facts upon which your conclusions are based. Now if your report has facts rather than opinions, the person for whom the report is intended need not agree with your conclusions or recommendations. That is not always necessary, for at least he has the facts by which to form his own conclusions and recommendations. You may give two persons exactly the same set of facts. One person may come to one conclusion; the second person to another. There can be disagreement about conclusions, but there should be no disagreement about facts.

Suppose your supervisor has called on you to write a report about a person under your supervision. You have had a great deal of trouble, including personal trouble, with this individual, and hastily you write a report. "She comes in too late. She takes too much time for lunch. She has proved herself to be very inefficient. I recommend that her services be dispensed with." Have you given facts or opinions? You have given only opinions. What are the facts? We can make an investigation. We study the time sheets. January 2, came in at 9:05; January 3, came in at 9:07; January 22, came in at 9:22. Then check back on her lunch times. She is permitted a half hour for lunch. January 2, was out from 12:00 to 12:50; January 3, out from 12:30 to 1:15. On the basis of those facts, you can conclude that this particular person has been negligent. She has disobeyed the rules. She is not worthy of being employed here. Your conclusions would then seem much sounder than they would if the facts had not been presented. So, it is the facts that make a report. If you don't have facts, you don't have a report. You just have a set of opinions and unwarranted recommendations.

ORGANIZATION

What is the next big step in writing a report? The next step is that of organization. You have to arrange your material. What we want to do now is to interpret or analyze the problem. To analyze means to break down or to divide. You have heard the expression, "To divide is to conquer." Well, divide a report problem and you conquer it.

Well, we have accomplished this much: We have investigated, we have arranged, we have done everything but write the report. That is another problem. In writing the report, we have got to appear unbiased, of course. We must be as logical in the report proper as we were in our outline; but, more than that, we have got to make ourselves clear.

EXAMPLES OF OUTLINE HEADINGS

A. Basic Three-part Type.

The simplest form of outline and the one most used is comprised of three major headings—

1. Introduction
   (Statement of topic or problem; brief background)

2. Body
   (The real information to be transmitted under headings and subheadings)

   a.
      (1)
      (2)

   b.
      (1)
      (2)

   c.
      (1)
      (2)

3. Conclusion
   (Very concise statement to indicate how the above facts answer the basic question or contribute to better understanding of the subject)

B. Staff Study Type.

A format often used in the Army; subject to considerable variation.

1. The Problem

   a.

   b.

2. Facts Bearing on the Situation
   (history)

   a.
      (1)
      (2)

   b.
      (1)
      (2)

3. Present Situation

   a.

   b.

4. Proposed Actions

   a.
      (1)
      (2)

   b.
      (1)
      (2)

5. Conclusion

QUESTIONS ON PREPARING REPORTS

1. As supervisor of a stenographic unit, you assign one of your stenographers to type a long, complicated report. After she begins work on the report, she asks you to explain the procedure to be followed in preparing a part of the report. You explain the procedure, but realize later that you have omitted instructions which she should have been given. Of the following, the most appropriate action for you to take in this situation is to:

   (A) state that you gave her incomplete instructions and supply her with the instructions you omitted
   (B) suggest, without referring to your omission, that she use her judgment in handling problems not covered by your instructions
   (C) supply her with the additional instructions when it becomes apparent that she is preparing the report incorrectly
   (D) assure the stenographer that you will answer any further questions she may have about this assignment.

2. "Internal management reporting in government agencies is becoming more statistical in nature. Statistics have thus become a major tool in management supervision in public agencies." Before deciding to adopt statistical reporting as a management tool, the management of a public agency should first determine whether the:

   (A) employees of the agency understand the need for, and the use of, statistics in reporting
   (B) supervisory staff in the agency is capable of putting reports into statistical form
   (C) major activities of the agency can be reported statistically
   (D) present achievements of the agency can be compared statistically with those of previous years.

3. "As an organization grows larger, the amount of personal contact between the top administrative officials and the rank and file employees diminishes. Consequently, management comes to rely more heavily upon written reports and records for securing information and exercising control." The most valid implication of this quotation is that, as an organization grows larger:

   (A) evaluation of the work of rank and file employees becomes more objective because of greater reliance upon written reports and records
   (B) relations between first line supervisors and their subordinates grow more impersonal
   (C) top administrative officials depend upon less direct methods for controlling the work of their subordinates
   (D) it becomes more difficult for top administrative officials to maintain high morale among rank and file employees.

4. Assume that your supervisor has asked you to present comprehensive, periodic reports on the progress that your unit is making in meeting its work goals. For you to give your superior oral reports rather than written ones is:

   (A) desirable; it will be easier for your superior to transmit your oral reports to his or her superiors
   (B) undesirable; the oral reports will provide no permanent record for reference
   (C) undesirable; there will be less opportunity for you to discuss the oral reports than the written ones
   (D) desirable; the oral reports will require little time and effort to prepare.

5. The head of a central transcribing unit has prepared monthly reports of the total amount of work performed by her unit. An analysis of the monthly reports for twenty-four successive months would be of least value to the unit head in:

   (A) anticipating peak work load periods
   (B) determining the quality of work which she can expect each employee to perform in the future
   (C) determining future personnel needs
   (D) estimating the amount of supplies that will be needed for the ensuing year.

6. "The total numbers of errors made during the month, or other period studied, indicates, in a general way, whether the work has been performed with reasonable accuracy. However, this is not in itself a true measure, but must be considered in relation to the total volume of work produced." On the basis of this quotation, the accuracy of work performed in a certain stenographic unit is most truly measured by the:

(A) total number of errors made during a specified period
(B) comparison of the number of errors made during one month with the number made during the preceding month
(C) ratio between the number of errors made and the quantity of work produced during a specified period
(D) average amount of work produced by the unit during each month or other designated period of time.

Answer questions 7, 8 and 9 on the basis of the following paragraph:

The supervisor of a large clerical and statistical division has assigned to one of the units under his supervision the preparation of a special statistical report required by the department head. The unit head accepted the assignment without comment but soon ran into considerable difficulty because no one in his unit had had any statistical training.

7. If a result of this lack of training is that the report is not completed on time, although everyone has done all that could be expected, the ultimate responsibility for the failure rests with:
(A) the department head
(B) the supervisor
(C) the unit head
(D) the employees in the unit.

8. This indicates that the supervisory staff has insufficient knowledge of employee:
(A) capabilities
(B) reaction to increased demands
(C) on-the-job training needs
(D) ability to perform ordinary assignments.

9. After working on the report for two days, the unit head notifies the supervisor that he will not be able to get the report out in the re-quired time. He states that his staff will be completely trained in another day or two and that after that preparing the report will be a simple matter. At this stage the supervisor decides to have the statistical unit prepare the report. This action on the part of the supervisor is:

(A) undesirable; the unit head should be given an incentive to continue with his training program which may produce good results
(B) desirable; it is the most efficient way in which the supervisor can show his displeasure with the unit head's failure
(C) undesirable; it may adversely affect the morale of the unit
(D) desirable; it will generally result in a better report completed in a shorter time.

10. "Reports submitted to the department head should be complete to the last detail. As far as possible, summaries should be avoided." This statement is, in general:

(A) correct; only on the basis of complete information can a proper decision be reached
(B) not correct; if all reports submitted were of this character a department head would never complete the work
(C) correct; the decision as to what is important and what is not can only be made by the person who is responsible for the action
(D) not correct; preliminary reports, obviously, cannot be complete to the last detail.

11. The one of the following which is NOT an essential element of an integrated reporting system for work-measurement is a:

(A) uniform record form for accumulating data and instruction for its maintenance
(B) procedure for routing reports upward through the organization and routing summaries downward
(C) looseleaf revisable manual which contains all procedural materials that are reasonably permanent and have a substantial reference value
(D) method for summarizing, analyzing and presenting data from several reports.

12. "Constant study should be made of the information contained in reports to isolate those elements of experience which are static, those which are variable and repetitive, and those which are variable and due to chance." Knowledge of those elements of experience in his organization which are static or constant will enable the operating official to:

(A) fix responsibility for their supervision at a lower level
(B) revise the procedure in order to make the elements variable
(C) arrange for a follow-up and periodic adjustment
(D) bring related data together.

13. During a conference of administrative staff personnel, the department head discussing the letters prepared for his signature stated, "Use no more words than are necessary to express your meaning." Following this rule in letter writing is, in general:

(A) desirable; considerable time will be saved in the preparation of correspondence
(B) undesirable; it is frequently necessary to elaborate on an explanation in order to made certain that the reader will understand
(C) desirable; the use of more words than are necessary is likely to obscure the meaning and tire the reader

(D) undesirable; terse statements are generally cold and formal and produce an unfavorable reaction in the reader.

14. You are preparing a long report addressed to your superior on a study which you have conducted. The one of the following sections which should come first in the report is a:

(A) description of the working procedure utilized in the study
(B) description of the situation which exists
(C) summary of the conclusions of the survey
(D) discussion of possible objections to the report and their refutation.

15. "Reported information is not needed at levels higher than those at which decisions are made on the basis of the information reported." This statement is, in general

(A) correct; if no action is to be taken on the basis of the information, the information is unnecessary
(B) not correct; all information is of importance in arriving at a sound decision
(C) correct; levels below the one at which the decision is made have need of the information
(D) not correct; levels below the one at which the decision is made do not have need of the information.

Answer Key

1. A	6. C	11. C
2. D	7. B	12. A
3. C	8. A	13. C
4. B	9. D	14. C
5. B	10. B	15. A

GLOSSARY OF LEGAL TERMS

This is some of the language you're likely to see on your examination. You may not need to know all the words in this carefully prepared glossary, but if even a few appear, you'll be that much ahead of your competitors. Perhaps the greater benefit from this list is the frame of mind it can create for you. Without reading a lot of technical text you'll steep yourself in just the right atmosphere for high test marks.

[A]

a posteriori from effect to cause.

a priori from cause to effect.

ab initio from the beginning.

abate destroy; remove.

abet encourage; aid.

abjure renounce.

abridge reduce; contract.

abrogate repeal; annul.

abscond hide; absent one's self.

accident unforseen event.

accomplice associate in crime.

acknowledgment act of going before an authorized official to declare an act as one's own, thus giving it legal validity.

acquit release; absolve.

act something done voluntarily.

ad litem for the suit.

adduce offer; present.

adjacent near to; close.

adjective law rules of procedure.

adjudicate to determine judicially.

admiralty court having jurisdiction over maritime cases.

adolescent boys 14 to 21; girls 12 to 21.

adult one who has attained the age of majority or legal maturity.

affiant one who makes an affidavit.

affidavit a sworn, written statement.

affiliation order stating one to be the father of a child.

affinity relationship between persons through marriage with the kindred of each other; distinguished from consanguinity which is relationship by blood.

affirm ratify.

affirmation a solemn declaration made under penalty of perjury by a person who conscientiously declines taking an oath.

agent one who represents and acts for another.

aggressor one who begins a quarrel.

aid and comfort help; encourage.

alias a name that is not one's true name.

alibi a claim of not being present at a certain place at a certain time.

alienist a doctor specializing in legal aspects of psychiatry.

allegation the assertion, declaration, or statement of a party to an action, made in a pleading, setting out what he expects to prove.

ambiguous not clear, having two meanings; equivocal.

amentia mental deficiency.

amercement a pecuniary penalty or a fine imposed as punishment on conviction.

amicus curiae a friend of the court who advises on some legal matter.

animus mind; intent.

animus furandi intent to steal.

annul cancel; void.

annus a year.

ante before.

ante mortem before death.

aphasia inability to speak although vocal cords are normal.

appeal to request a higher court to review a decision of a lower court.

appearance the coming into court as defendant, attorney, etc.

appellant one who appeals.

appellee one who opposes an appellant; a respondent.

apprehend arrest.

appurtenant belonging to.

arbiter one who decides a dispute; a referee.

arbitrary an act having no cause or reason; absolute; despotic; peremptory.

arraign to call a prisoner before the court to answer to a charge.

artifice trickery; deception.

asportation moving a thing from one place to another as in larceny.

assert to state as true.

asseveration an affirmation; a solemn declaration.

asylum a place of refuge.

at bar before the court.

at issue the point of contention between parties in a legal action.

attach seize property by court order and sometimes arrest a person.

attainder forfeiture of property and corruption of honor of one sentenced to death. (Compare with *bill of attainder* below.)

attempt an act done with intent to commit a crime but falling short of consummating it.

attest to witness a will, etc.

authentic genuine; true.

authenticate to give authority to a law, writing, or record.

axio a self-evident truth.

[B]

bail   the security given to obtain the temporary release of a prisoner.

bailee   one to whom goods are bailed.

bailment   the giving of property to a bailee.

bailor   the one who gives his property to a bailee.

barratry   the persistent incitement of groundless judicial proceedings.

battery   illegal interfering with another's person.

bill of attainder   a law pronouncing a person guilty without trial. It is illegal.

bludgeon   a club heavier at one end than at the other.

blue laws   rigid Sunday laws.

blue-sky laws   laws regulating investment companies to protect investors from frauds.

bona fide   in good faith.

bondsman   one who bails another by putting up a bond.

boycott   a plan to prevent the carrying on of a business by wrongful means.

breach of the peace   disturbing the public peace by disorder, violence, force, noise, etc.

bucket shop   a place where people bet on the stock market under pretense of buying and selling stocks.

bunco game   any trick or cunning calculated to win confidence and to deceive whether by conversation, conduct, or suggestion.

[C]

cadaver   a dead human body.

camera   a judge's chamber.

canon   a law; rule.

capias   an order to arrest.

carnal   relating to the body.

carnal abuse   a sex act not amounting to penetration.

carnal knowledge   sexual intercourse.

cause of action   matter for which an action may be brought.

caveat   let him beware.

caveat emptor   let the buyer beware.

certiorari   an order from a high court to a lower court calling up for review the minutes of a trial.

challenge   an exception taken to a juror.

change of venue   the removal of the place of trial from one county to another.

character   the qualities or traits that make up or distinguish an individual.

charge   a complaint, information or indictment.

chastity   abstention from unlawful sexual intercourse.

chattel personal property.

chattel mortgage a mortgage on personal property.

child one under 16 years in criminal law.

cite to summon; command one's presence.

civil rights rights granted to citizens by the Constitution or by statute.

codicil an addition to a will.

coercion compulsion, duress.

cognomen a family name.

cohabit to live together as husband and wife.

comity courtesy, respect; agreement between states to recognize each other's laws.

commitment an order to take one to prison.

common law law as it developed in England based on customs, usage, decisions, etc.

commute change punishment to one less severe.

complainant one who seeks legal redress.

complaint a sworn allegation to a magistrate charging one with crime. Also called information.

compos mentis sound of mind.

compromise an agreement between one charged with certain crimes and the complainant to withdraw charges on payment of money, with court's consent.

concubinage habitual cohabitation of persons not legally married.

concurrent occurring at the same time.

condemnation taking private property for public use on payment thereof.

confess to admit the truth of a charge.

confession voluntary statement of guilt of a crime.

confidence game a swindle.

confrontation the right of the defendant to have the witness stand face-to-face with the defendant when the accusation is made.

connivance secret or indirect consent by one to a criminal act by another.

consanguinity blood relationship.

consecutive successive.

conspiracy a plan by two or more to commit a crime.

constitution the fundamental law of a state or nation.

constructive intent if one intends one act and in carrying it out does another, the intent to do the first is construed to apply to the second.

contiguous near by.

contingency an event that may or may not happen.

contra against.

contraband illegal or prohibited traffic.

controvert to dispute or oppose by reasoning.

conviction judgment that one is guilty as charged.

corporal bodily.

corpus delicti the substantial and fundamental fact necessary to prove a crime.

corroborate to strengthen.

corrupt spoiled, tainted, debased.

counselor a lawyer.

counterfeit to forge, copy, imitate.

credible worthy of belief.

crimen falsi crimes involving deceit or falsification.

criminal action the process by which one is accused of a crime and brought to trial and punishment.

criminal information same as complaint.

criminal intent intent to commit crime.

criminology the scientific study of crime, criminals and penal treatment.

culpable blamable.

cumulative tending to prove the same point in evidence; increasing severity with repetition of the offense.

curtilage ground adjacent to a dwelling and used in connection with it. Usually this space is fenced off.

custody control exercised by legal authority over a ward or suspect.

[D]

deadly weapon an instrument likely to produce death or serious bodily injury.

debauch to corrupt by intemperance or sensuality.

decision a judgment rendered by a proper court.

deed a signed instrument containing a legal transfer, bargain or contract.

defalcation the act or instance of embezzling.

de facto actually or really existing.

defamation injuring a reputation by false statements.

defendant one who defends or denies a charge.

defraud to deprive of property by fraud or deceit.

de jure by right of law.

deliberate to weigh or ponder before forming a decision.

delict an offense against the law.

demented mad or insane.

deponent one who gives written testimony under oath.

deposition sworn written testimony.

design plan, scheme, intent.

dictum an opinion on a point in a case expressed by a judge.

dipsomaniac one who has an irresistible desire for alcohol.

disfranchise to deprive of a legal right.

dismiss to discharge a court action.

disorderly house a place where people behave so badly as to become a nuisance to the neighborhood.

document a written instrument.

domicile one's permanent home.

duress forcible restraint.

[E]

ego   the self.

eleemosynary   related to or supported by charity.

embezzlement   appropriation of entrusted property fraudulently for one's own use.

embracery   an attempt to influence a juror improperly.

eminent domain   the right of a government to take private property for public use.

empirical   based on experience.

entice   to solicit, persuade, allure by flattery, coaxing, etc.

entrapment   the act of luring one into a compromising statement or act.

essence   the ultimate nature of a thing.

evidence   all means used to prove or disprove a fact in issue.

ex officio   by virtue of office.

ex parte   on one side only.

ex post facto law   a law passed after an act was done which retroactively makes such an act a crime.

examined copy   one compared with the original and sworn to as a correct copy.

exception   a formal objection to the action of the court in denying a request or overruling an objection.

executed   completed.

extradition   surrender of a fugitive from one nation to another.

extrajudicial   outside judicial proceeding.

extremis   near death, beyond hope of recovery.

[F]

facsimile   an exact or accurate copy of an original instrument.

false pretenses   intentionally untrue representations.

felo de se   one who kills himself; suicide.

felonious   criminal, malicious.

fence   one who buys stolen property.

fiduciary   holding in trust.

filiation, order of   a court order declaring one to be the father of an illegitimate child.

finding   the result of the deliberation of a court or jury.

firearm   a weapon that propels bullets by explosion of gunpowder.

forge   to counterfeit or make falsely.

fornication   sexual intercourse between persons not married to each other.

foundling   a deserted child.

franchise   a special privilege granted to an individual or group; elective franchise refers to the voting privilege.

fratricide   killing of one's brother or sister.

freeholder   one who owns real property.

fugitive from justice   one who commits a crime in one state and goes to another.

[G]

gamble   to bet on an event of which the outcome is uncertain.

general verdict   a verdict in which a jury finds a defendant guilty or not guilty.

genocide   the deliberate systematic destruction of certain races, nationalities or religious groups.

gift enterprise   a scheme for distribution of property by chance among persons who have paid or agreed to pay a consideration; the common term is lottery.

grand jury   not less than 16 but no more than 23 citizens of a county sworn to inquire into crimes committed or triable in that county.

grantee   one to whom a grant is made.

grantor   the one who makes the grant.

gravamen   the substantial part of a complaint.

guardian ad litem   a person designated by a court to represent a child bringing or defending a civil action.

[H]

habeas corpus   an order to produce a person before a court to determine the legality of detention.

hearsay   evidence based on repeating the words told by another and not based on the witness's own personal observation or knowledge of that to which he testifies.

hung jury   one so divided they can't agree on a verdict.

hypothecate   to pledge without delivery of title or possession.

hypothetical question   a question asked of an expert witness based on supposition from which the witness is asked to state his opinion.

[I]

illicit   unlawful.

impeach   to accuse, charge.

inalienable   those rights which cannot be lawfully transferred or surrendered.

in loco parentis   in place of a parent.

incommunicado   denial of the right of a prisoner to communicate with friends or relatives.

indictment   a written accusation of a crime presented by a grand jury.

inducement cause or reason why a thing is done or that which incites the person to do the act or commit a crime; the motive for the criminal act.

infamous crime a felony.

infant in civil cases one under 21 years of age.

information a formal accusation of a crime.

injunction legal process requiring a person to do or refrain from doing a certain action.

intent state of mind to do or omit an act.

ipso facto by the fact itself.

issue what is affirmed by one and denied by another in an action.

[J]

jeopardy danger, peril.

judicial notice acceptance by a court or judge of some fact of common knowledge thereby dispensing with the need of offering evidence to prove it; i.e., 24 hours equal one day.

judiciary relating to a court of justice.

jurat the part of an affidavit stating where, when and before whom it was signed and sworn.

jurisdiction power or authority to apply or interpret the law.

jury a group of citizens sworn to inquire into facts and deliver a verdict. A trial jury (generally 12) tries cases; a grand jury (generally 23) indicts.

[K]

kleptomaniac one who has an irresistable propensity to steal.

[L]

laches unreasonable delay in asserting a legal right or privelege.

latent hidden, concealed.

leading question one so put as to suggest the answer.

lien a claim a creditor has on property until a debt is paid.

lis pendens a pending civil or criminal action.

litigant a party to a lawsuit.

locus delicti place of the crime.

locus poenitentiae the abandoning or giving up of one's intention to commit some crime before it is fully completed, or abandoning a conspiracy before its purpose is accomplished.

lucri causa for sake of gain.

[M]

mala in se   bad in themselves; such crimes usually require a specific criminal intent.

mala prohibita   bad because it is prohibited by legislation, not because it is evil in its nature.

malfeasance   wrongdoing or misconduct, especially by a public official.

malice-intentional   wrongdoing to injure, vex or annoy.

malo animo   evil mind.

mandamus   a court order to a public official to perform a specified act.

maritime   pertaining to the sea or to commerce thereon.

masochism   sexual pleasure in being abused or dominated.

mens rea   criminal intent.

meretricious   relating to a prostitute.

minor   one who has not attained majority.

miscegenation   marriage or sexual intercourse between persons of different races.

misfeasance   improper performance of a lawful act.

mittimus   a warrant of commitment to prison.

moral certainty   evidence which convinces the mind beyond a reasonable doubt; hence the degree of proof required to prove defendant's guilt in a criminal action.

moral turpitude   base or vile behavior.

motive   reason for doing an act.

mulct   a pecuniary fine imposed as punishment upon conviction of a crime; same as amercement.

[N]

natural child   a child born out of wedlock.

nolle prosequi   an entry of record signifying that the plaintiff or prosecutor will not press the complaint.

nolo contendere   equal to a plea of guilty.

nominal damages   award of a trifling sum where no substantial injury is proved to have been sustained.

nonfeasance   neglect of duty.

noscitur a sociis   meaning of doubtful words in a statute may be ascertained by referring to the meaning of other words associated with it in the definition; also called *ejusdem generis*.

novation   substitution of a new obligation for an old one.

nunc pro tunc   now for then; dated as if occuring on an earlier date.

[O]

oath   an attestation of the truth.

obiter dictum   opinion expressed by a court on a matter not essentially involved in a case and hence not a decision; also called *dicta* if plural.

onus probandi   burden of proof.

opinion evidence   inferences or conclusions stated by a witness in testimony as distinguished from facts known to him; generally inadmissible.

overt   open, manifest.

[P]

panel   a group of jurors selected to serve during a term of the court.

pardon   to release an offender from punishment for his crime.

parens patriae   sovereign power of a state to protect or be a guardian over children and incompetents.

parol   oral, verbal.

parole   to release one from prison conditionally before the expiration of his sentence.

peculation   embezzlement.

petit treason   common law crime in which a wife kills her husband, or a servant kills his master, or a subordinate kills his superior. Abolished as such under N.Y. Statute law when all such killings were classified as criminal homicides.

police power   inherent power of the state or its political subdivisions to enact laws within constitutional limits to promote the general welfare of society or the community.

polling the jury   calling the names of persons on a jury and requiring each juror to declare what his verdict is before it is legally recorded.

post mortem   after death.

power of attorney   an instrument authorizing one to act for another.

premeditate   to think or consider beforehand.

presentment   a report by a grand jury of an offense from their own knowledge, without any bill of indictment.

presumption   an inference as to the existence of some fact not known arising from its connection with facts which exist or are known to exist.

prima facie   at first sight.

prima facie case   a case where the evidence is very strong against the defendant.

primary evidence   term applied to originals of written documents when placed in evidence.

pro and con   for and against.

probation   release of one after conviction, conditionally, without confining him in prison.

probative   tending to prove.

[Q]

quasi crime   violations of law not constituting crimes but punishable as wrongs against the local or general public welfare; thus, minor offenses.

quo warranto   a legal procedure to test an official's right to a public office or the right to hold a franchise, or to hold an office in a domestic corporation.

[R]

reasonable   fit and appropriate.

reasonable doubt   a doubt regarding the guilt of the accused person which entitles him to an acquittal.

rebuttal   evidence to the contrary.

recidivist   habitual criminal.

recognizance   a written statement before a court to do an act specified or to suffer a penalty.

recrimination   accusation made by an accused person against his accuser.

rehabilitate   to reform.

remand   to send a prisoner back to jail after a hearing.

removal   a federal procedure by which a fugitive from justice under U.S. laws is returned for trial to the federal district wherein he committed his crime. May also refer to removing the trial for a criminal action from one county to another county or to another court.

replevin   an action to recover goods unlawfully taken or withheld.

rescission   annulment of a contract.

respondeat superior   general rule charging the master or employer with liability for his servant's or employee's negligence in an act causing injury to third persons.

res adjudicata   doctrine that an issue or dispute litigated and determined in a case between opposing parties is deemed permanently decided between these parties.

[S]

scienter   allegation that the defendant had knowledge or willfully committed the crime with which he is charged.

special verdict   a verdict written by the jury which finds the facts only, leaving the legal judgment to the judge.

situs delicti   the place where a crime originates. (See *locus delicti*.)

stare decisis   general rule that when an issue has been settled by a court decision, it forms a precedent which is not to be departed from in deciding similar future issues.

struck jury a special jury or a blue ribbon jury.

suborn to induce to commit perjury.

subpoena a court process requiring one to appear as a witness.

subpoena duces tecum a subpoena to produce records, books and documents.

subrogation substitution of one person for another in respect to rights and claims, debts, etc.

sui generis of the same kind. (See *noscitur a sociis*.)

summons a court order requesting one to appear to answer a charge.

surety a bondsman.

surname a family name.

suspend sentence hold back a sentence pending a prisoner's good behavior.

[T]

talesman person summoned to fill a panel of jurors when the regular panel is exhausted.

testimony spoken or written evidence.

tolling the statute facts which remove the statute of limitations as a bar to a criminal prosecution.

tort a breach of legal duty caused by a wrongful act or neglect resulting in injury or loss for which the injured party may sue for damages.

trespass illegal entry into another's property.

true bill indictment.

trustee one who lawfully holds property in custody for the benefit of another.

turpitude anything done contrary to justice, honesty, morals; same as moral turpitude.

[U]

undertaking a written agreement to appear in court when released on bail.

usury unlawful interest on a loan.

[V]

veniremen persons ordered to appear to serve on a jury or composing a panel of jurors.

venue the place or location where the cause of legal action arises.

verdict the findings of a jury; decision is the finding by a judge.

vi et armis phrase used in indictments and information indicating the crime was committed with force, by violence, weapons, etc.

voir dire preliminary examination of a witness or a juror to test competency, etc.

[W]

waive   to give up a right.

warrant   a written court order given to a peace officer to arrest the one named in it.

[Z]

zoning laws   laws specifying the use to which land in a city may be put; for example, residential, commercial, industrial, etc. May regulate height, width, and size of structures in a certain district. It is justified as a form of police power by the city or state.

LAW BOOKS

Law Dictionaries   Bouvier; Black; Ballentine

Law of Evidence   Richardson; Wigmore; Wharton; McKelvey

Annual Session Laws of N.Y.   McKinney

Consolidated and Unconsolidated Laws of N.Y.   McKinney

Civil Practice Act; Rules of Civil Procedure; Civil Courts Acts; Rules of Civic Courts   Clevenger Practice Manual

Penal Law and Code of Criminal Procedure   McKinney; Gilbert

CHARGING THE SUSPECT

The following exercise involves the comprehension of the elements of various crimes that a state trooper encounters frequently while performing the duties of the position and the proper charging of a suspect based on the information contained in the questions that follow.

DEFINITIONS OF CRIMES LISTED ALPHABETICALLY

Arson is committed when an individual intentionally starts a fire that causes damage to a building or ignites an explosion.

Assault is committed when a person causes physical injury with intent to another person, or when a person, acting recklessly, causes physical injury to another person.

Burglary is committed when an individual, without authorization, enters or remains in a building with the intent of committing a crime.

Criminal Mischief is committed when a person intentionally damages the property of another person, having no right to do so, nor any reasonable ground to believe that he or she has the right to do so.

Criminal Trespass is committed when a person enters or remains in a building he or she has no right to be in and, while there, possesses, or has knowledge of another person accompanying him possessing, a weapon.

Criminally Negligent Homicide is committed when the behavior of an individual creates a substantial risk for others and results in the unintentional death of a person.

Felony Murder is committed when a person, acting alone or with others, commits or attempts to commit the crimes of robbery, burglary, kidnapping, arson, or rape and in the course of furtherance of such crime, or immediate flight therefrom, that person, or another participant, if there be any, causes the death of a person other than one of the participants.

Harassment is committed when an individual, with intent to annoy of frighten another individual, does strike, shove, kick or subject that individual to physical contact, or attempts or threatens to do the same, or uses abusive or obscene language, or makes an obscene gesture in a public place, or follows a person in a public place, or repeatedly engages in conduct which serves no legitimate purpose, but which results in alarming or seriously annoying another person.

Jostling is committed when a person, with intent, unnecessarily places a hand near a person's pocket or handbag, or pushes or crowds another person at the same time that another participant's hand is in the proximity of such person's pocket or handbag.

Larceny is committed when a person intentionally deprives another of property or wrongfully takes, obtains, or withholds property from the owner of that property without the use of force, violence or threat of injury. Larceny is committed, for example, when property is obtained under false pretenses; finding and not returning lost property; or the intentional issuance of a bad check.

Manslaughter is committed when one person recklessly causes the death of another person; when a person causes the death of another person while in the act of intentionally causing serious harm to that person; when a person, intending to cause the death of another person, causes that death while acting under the influence of an extreme emotional disturbance.

Menace is committed when a person, by physical threat, intentionally places, or attempts to place, another person in a state of fear of imminent and serious physical injury.

Murder is committed when a person, following a period of lengthy planning, intentionally causes the death of another person.

Reckless Endangerment is committed when a person, failing to exercise caution, engages in conduct which creates a substantial risk of serious injury to another person.

Reckless Endangerment of Property is committed when a person, in the act of failing to exercise proper caution, engages in conduct which creates a risk of damage to the property of another person.

Robbery is committed when a person, against another person's will, takes property from that person.

Sexual Abuse is committed when one person subjects another person to sexual contact without the person's consent; or when one person has sexual contact with another person who has not reached their fourteenth birthday. "Sexual contact" involves touching another person' sexual or intimate parts for the purpose of achieving gratification of a sexual desire.

Sexual Misconduct is committed when a male has sexual intercourse with a female who has consented to the act and the female is at least thirteen years of age but has not yet reached her seventeenth birthday.

The following questions are to be answered on the basis of the preceding legal definitions of crimes. Although these definitions may vary slightly from state to state, you are to answer the questions solely on the basis of the definitions stated here.

1. Jane Wills finds a diamond ring on the sidewalk of a busy street. She keeps it. According to the definitions, Wills committed

   (A) the crime of larceny
   (B) the crime of burglary
   (C) none of the listed crimes
   (D) the crime of robbery

2. Ephriam Towne is waiting at a bus station to hand over a package of expensive jewelry to a representative of the XYZ Transfer Company. Phil Shute learns of the shipment and decides to steal the package. He goes to the bus station, presents himself to Towne, and says he is from XYZ. Towne gives Shute the package believing he is from XYZ. Shute is not armed. The definitions indicate that Shute committed the crime of

   (A) robbery
   (B) burglary
   (C) criminal mischief
   (D) larceny

3. Leo Charles tries out his new sports car. He drives 70 miles per hour on a school street during school hours and accidentally hits and kills a child. According to the legal definitions, Charles has committed the crime of

   (A) criminally negligent homicide
   (B) menacing
   (C) felony murder
   (D) murder

4. Conrad Hill and Leonard Burke are walking when they pass a museum. It is late at night, long after the museum ordinarily closes to the public. Hill notices that the front door is open and he suggests that they go in and have a private visit of the museum as a prank. Hill happens to have a flashlight with him. Unknown to Hill, Burke has a concealed gun on his person that is an illegal weapon. Ten minutes after they have entered the museum the two men hear footsteps approaching. They dash out of the museum the same way they had entered it. According to the definitions given,

   (A) both Hill and Burke committed the crime of criminal trespass
   (B) neither Hill nor Burke committed the crime of criminal trespass
   (C) Burke committed the crime of criminal trespass; Hill did not
   (D) Hill committed the crime of criminal trespass; Burke did not

5. Which one of the following is the best example of a burglary based upon the definitions given?

    (A) Mr. Samuel's car breaks down in the middle of the night while he is driving on a lonely road. He locates a nearby house which is unoccupied in order to find shelter from the rain.
    (B) During working hours, Wilson, a mechanic, enters the locker room of the factory where he is employed and steals tools from another mechanic's locker.
    (C) Burns, a teenager, passes the open door of a warehouse. He does not see anybody inside the warehouse but he notices a portable radio on a desk. He enters the warehouse with the intention of stealing the radio but before he can do so he hears approaching footsteps and he leaves without taking anything.
    (D) Mr. Jurow enters a drug store with the intention of purchasing some toothpaste. The clerk is busy at the back of the store. Jurow, spotting the toothpaste he wants, removes it from the shelf, puts it in his pocket and leaves.

6. As a result of an argument over a parking space, Anne Blount and Bea Wallace engage in an argument during which Blount pushes Wallace in an attempt to scare her. Wallace is not hurt, but she makes an obscene gesture in the direction of Blount. Referring to the definitions given, which one of the following best describes the incident?

    (A) Blount committed assault and Wallace committed harassment
    (B) Blount and Wallace both committed harassment
    (C) Neither Blount nor Wallace committed harassment
    (D) Wallace committed assault and Blount committed harassment

7. William Hammer, fully intending to scare James Bates, drives his car at high speed in the direction of Bates who quickly jumps out of the path of the vehicle. In turning in the direction of Bates, Hammer narrowly misses Fred Collins, a bystander. Neither Bates nor Collins is injured. According to the definitions, Hammer

    (A) did not commit an assault against Bates or Collins
    (B) did not commit a crime
    (C) committed an assault against Bates and Collins
    (D) committed an assault against Collins only

8. Jon Ochtes picks the pocket of Will Ronge and takes his wallet. Ronge is unaware that his wallet has been taken. Referring to the definitions, Ochtes committed the crime of

    (A) robbery
    (B) burglary
    (C) larceny
    (D) criminal trespass

9. James Calvin is driving his car and has as his passenger his four-year old daughter Pamela. Calvin's car is suddenly struck by another car and as a result of the accident Pamela is instantly killed. Calvin, upon learning of his daughter's death, approaches the driver of the other vehicle, takes out a gun and shoots him dead. The definitions indicate that Calvin had committed the crime of

   (A) felony murder
   (B) criminally negligent homicide
   (C) murder
   (D) manslaughter

10. James Floyd has an argument with John Rudd. Floyd then sets fire to Rudd's car, totally destroying it. According to the definitions given, James Floyd has committed the crime of

   (A) arson
   (B) criminal mischief
   (C) reckless endangerment of property
   (D) harassment

11. Roger Brown enjoys, and engages in, the practice of making obscene gestures towards passengers on subway trains. According to the definitions given, when Brown is in the act of making obscene gestures, he is committing the crime of

   (A) menace
   (B) jostling
   (C) reckless endangerment
   (D) harassment

Answer Key

1. A	5. C	9. D
2. D	6. B	10. B
3. A	7. A	11. D
4. C	8. C	

PART FIVE

Final Sample Practice Examination

5

State Trooper

FINAL SAMPLE PRACTICE EXAMINATION

This professionally-constructed Examination is unique. It is not a copy of previous exams nor of the forthcoming exam. The actual exams are closely guarded, secure; and may not be duplicated. The exam you'll take may have more difficult questions in some areas than you'll encounter on this Sample Examination. On the other hand, some questions may be easier, but don't bank on it. We mean to give you confidence . . . not over-confidence.

Time allowed for the entire Examination: 3 Hours

ANSWER SHEET FOR SAMPLE FINAL PRACTICE EXAMINATION

TEST I. JUDGMENT AND REASONING

1 Ⓐ Ⓑ Ⓒ Ⓓ	4 Ⓐ Ⓑ Ⓒ Ⓓ	7 Ⓐ Ⓑ Ⓒ Ⓓ	10 Ⓐ Ⓑ Ⓒ Ⓓ	13 Ⓐ Ⓑ Ⓒ Ⓓ
2 Ⓐ Ⓑ Ⓒ Ⓓ	5 Ⓐ Ⓑ Ⓒ Ⓓ	8 Ⓐ Ⓑ Ⓒ Ⓓ	11 Ⓐ Ⓑ Ⓒ Ⓓ	14 Ⓐ Ⓑ Ⓒ Ⓓ
3 Ⓐ Ⓑ Ⓒ Ⓓ	6 Ⓐ Ⓑ Ⓒ Ⓓ	9 Ⓐ Ⓑ Ⓒ Ⓓ	12 Ⓐ Ⓑ Ⓒ Ⓓ	15 Ⓐ Ⓑ Ⓒ Ⓓ

TEST II. JUDGMENT AND REASONING

1 Ⓐ Ⓑ Ⓒ Ⓓ	4 Ⓐ Ⓑ Ⓒ Ⓓ	7 Ⓐ Ⓑ Ⓒ Ⓓ	10 Ⓐ Ⓑ Ⓒ Ⓓ	13 Ⓐ Ⓑ Ⓒ Ⓓ
2 Ⓐ Ⓑ Ⓒ Ⓓ	5 Ⓐ Ⓑ Ⓒ Ⓓ	8 Ⓐ Ⓑ Ⓒ Ⓓ	11 Ⓐ Ⓑ Ⓒ Ⓓ	14 Ⓐ Ⓑ Ⓒ Ⓓ
3 Ⓐ Ⓑ Ⓒ Ⓓ	6 Ⓐ Ⓑ Ⓒ Ⓓ	9 Ⓐ Ⓑ Ⓒ Ⓓ	12 Ⓐ Ⓑ Ⓒ Ⓓ	15 Ⓐ Ⓑ Ⓒ Ⓓ

TEST III. JUDGMENT AND REASONING

1 Ⓣ Ⓕ	5 Ⓣ Ⓕ	9 Ⓣ Ⓕ	13 Ⓣ Ⓕ	17 Ⓣ Ⓕ	21 Ⓣ Ⓕ	25 Ⓣ Ⓕ	29 Ⓣ Ⓕ
2 Ⓣ Ⓕ	6 Ⓣ Ⓕ	10 Ⓣ Ⓕ	14 Ⓣ Ⓕ	18 Ⓣ Ⓕ	22 Ⓣ Ⓕ	26 Ⓣ Ⓕ	30 Ⓣ Ⓕ
3 Ⓣ Ⓕ	7 Ⓣ Ⓕ	11 Ⓣ Ⓕ	15 Ⓣ Ⓕ	19 Ⓣ Ⓕ	23 Ⓣ Ⓕ	27 Ⓣ Ⓕ	31 Ⓣ Ⓕ
4 Ⓣ Ⓕ	8 Ⓣ Ⓕ	12 Ⓣ Ⓕ	16 Ⓣ Ⓕ	20 Ⓣ Ⓕ	24 Ⓣ Ⓕ	28 Ⓣ Ⓕ	

TEST IV. JUDGMENT AND REASONING

1 Ⓣ Ⓕ	7 Ⓣ Ⓕ	13 Ⓣ Ⓕ	19 Ⓣ Ⓕ	25 Ⓣ Ⓕ
2 Ⓣ Ⓕ	8 Ⓣ Ⓕ	14 Ⓣ Ⓕ	20 Ⓣ Ⓕ	26 Ⓣ Ⓕ
3 Ⓣ Ⓕ	9 Ⓣ Ⓕ	15 Ⓣ Ⓕ	21 Ⓣ Ⓕ	27 Ⓣ Ⓕ
4 Ⓣ Ⓕ	10 Ⓣ Ⓕ	16 Ⓣ Ⓕ	22 Ⓣ Ⓕ	28 Ⓣ Ⓕ
5 Ⓣ Ⓕ	11 Ⓣ Ⓕ	17 Ⓣ Ⓕ	23 Ⓣ Ⓕ	29 Ⓣ Ⓕ
6 Ⓣ Ⓕ	12 Ⓣ Ⓕ	18 Ⓣ Ⓕ	24 Ⓣ Ⓕ	30 Ⓣ Ⓕ

TEST V. READING COMPREHENSION AND INTERPRETATION

1 Ⓐ Ⓑ Ⓒ Ⓓ	4 Ⓐ Ⓑ Ⓒ Ⓓ	7 Ⓐ Ⓑ Ⓒ Ⓓ	10 Ⓐ Ⓑ Ⓒ Ⓓ	13 Ⓐ Ⓑ Ⓒ Ⓓ
2 Ⓐ Ⓑ Ⓒ Ⓓ	5 Ⓐ Ⓑ Ⓒ Ⓓ	8 Ⓐ Ⓑ Ⓒ Ⓓ	11 Ⓐ Ⓑ Ⓒ Ⓓ	14 Ⓐ Ⓑ Ⓒ Ⓓ
3 Ⓐ Ⓑ Ⓒ Ⓓ	6 Ⓐ Ⓑ Ⓒ Ⓓ	9 Ⓐ Ⓑ Ⓒ Ⓓ	12 Ⓐ Ⓑ Ⓒ Ⓓ	15 Ⓐ Ⓑ Ⓒ Ⓓ

TEST VI. READING COMPREHENSION AND INTERPRETATION

1 Ⓐ Ⓑ Ⓒ Ⓓ   6 Ⓐ Ⓑ Ⓒ Ⓓ   11 Ⓐ Ⓑ Ⓒ Ⓓ   16 Ⓐ Ⓑ Ⓒ Ⓓ

2 Ⓐ Ⓑ Ⓒ Ⓓ   7 Ⓐ Ⓑ Ⓒ Ⓓ   12 Ⓐ Ⓑ Ⓒ Ⓓ   17 Ⓐ Ⓑ Ⓒ Ⓓ

3 Ⓐ Ⓑ Ⓒ Ⓓ   8 Ⓐ Ⓑ Ⓒ Ⓓ   13 Ⓐ Ⓑ Ⓒ Ⓓ   18 Ⓐ Ⓑ Ⓒ Ⓓ

4 Ⓐ Ⓑ Ⓒ Ⓓ   9 Ⓐ Ⓑ Ⓒ Ⓓ   14 Ⓐ Ⓑ Ⓒ Ⓓ   19 Ⓐ Ⓑ Ⓒ Ⓓ

5 Ⓐ Ⓑ Ⓒ Ⓓ   10 Ⓐ Ⓑ Ⓒ Ⓓ   15 Ⓐ Ⓑ Ⓒ Ⓓ   20 Ⓐ Ⓑ Ⓒ Ⓓ

TEST VII. ARITHMETIC COMPUTATIONS

1 Ⓐ Ⓑ Ⓒ Ⓓ   4 Ⓐ Ⓑ Ⓒ Ⓓ   7 Ⓐ Ⓑ Ⓒ Ⓓ   10 Ⓐ Ⓑ Ⓒ Ⓓ   13 Ⓐ Ⓑ Ⓒ Ⓓ

2 Ⓐ Ⓑ Ⓒ Ⓓ   5 Ⓐ Ⓑ Ⓒ Ⓓ   8 Ⓐ Ⓑ Ⓒ Ⓓ   11 Ⓐ Ⓑ Ⓒ Ⓓ   14 Ⓐ Ⓑ Ⓒ Ⓓ

3 Ⓐ Ⓑ Ⓒ Ⓓ   6 Ⓐ Ⓑ Ⓒ Ⓓ   9 Ⓐ Ⓑ Ⓒ Ⓓ   12 Ⓐ Ⓑ Ⓒ Ⓓ

TEST 1. JUDGMENT AND REASONING

DIRECTIONS: For each question read all the lettered choices carefully. Then select that answer which you consider correct or most nearly correct and complete. Blacken the lettered space on your answer sheet corresponding to your best selection, just as you would have to do on the actual examination.

The answer key for this test will be found after the last test in this section.

1.　　　Suppose that, while on patrol late at night, you find a woman lying in the street, apparently the victim of a hit-and-run driver. She seems to be injured seriously but you wish to ask her one or two questions in order to help apprehend the hit-and-run car. Of the following, the best question to ask is:
(A) In what direction did the car go?
(B) What time did it happen?
(C) What kind of car was it?
(D) How many persons were in the car?

2.　　　"Driver 1 claimed that the collision occurred because, as he approached the intersection, Driver 2 started to make a left turn suddenly and at high speed, even though the light had been red against him for 15 or 20 seconds." Suppose that you have been assigned to make a report on this accident. The position of the vehicles after the accident is indicated in Figure 3, the point in each case indicating the front of the vehicle. On the basis of this sketch, the best reason for concluding that Driver 1's statement is false is that:

(A) Driver 2's car is beyond the center of the intersection
(B) Driver 2's car is making the turn on the proper side of the road
(C) Driver 1's car is beyond the sidewalk line
(D) Driver 1's car is on the right hand side of the road.

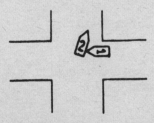

3.　　　"If possible, the principal witnesses, especially the most trustworthy ones, should be heard before the suspect is interrogated." The most valid reason for this procedure is that:

(A) the investigator will tend to be more adequately informed when questioning the suspect
(B) waiting to be questioned increases the pressure on the subject
(C) trustworthy witnesses tend to become untrustworthy if kept waiting
(D) all witnesses should be heard before the suspect.

4.　　　"It is important that the State Trooper establish the fact that the crime reported is bona fide." This procedure may best be evaluated as:

(A) necessary as many crimes are reported which have not taken place
(B) unnecessary as in only few cases are crimes simulated
(C) unnecessary as general investigation will show the nature of the crime without any emphasis on validity
(D) necessary as it gives the investigator a starting point.

5.　　　You are on your way to report for an assignment when you see two men fighting on the street. For you to attempt to stop the fight would be:

(A) unjustified; it is none of your business
(B) justified; a fight between individuals may turn into a riot
(C) unjustified; you may get hurt with the result that you will not be able to report for duty
(D) justified; as a peace officer it is your duty to see that the public peace is kept.

6.   **While patrolling your post you notice several people in two groups enter an old abandoned house by means of the rear entrance. The best action to take would be to:**
(A) call headquarters notifying your superior of the occurrence
(B) ignore the situation
(C) enter the house, gun drawn
(D) note the occurrence by an entry in your memorandum book.

7.   **"On a dark background bloodstains are often difficult to recognize. When searching for bloodstains in such cases, one should use a flashlight, even in the daytime." Of the following, the best reason for this procedure is that:**
(A) it is important to get as much light as possible
(B) the contrast around the edges of the light is great
(C) artificial light may make differentiation between the blood and the background possible
(D) the movement of the flashlight will cause a moving reflection.

8.   **Of the following kinds of wounds, the one in which there is the least danger of infection is:**
(A) an abrased wound
(B) a punctured wound
(C) a lacerated wound
(D) an incised wound.

9.   When a person is found injured on the street, it is generally advisable, pending arrival of a physician, to help prevent fainting or shock by keeping the patient:
(A) in a sitting position
(B) lying down with the head level
(C) lying down with the head raised
(D) standing up.

10.   When an injured person appears to be suffering from shock, of the

following, it is most essential to:
(A) loosen clothing
(B) keep the person warm
(C) administer a stimulant
(D) place the person in a prone position.

11.   **The one of the following statements made by a prisoner that is correctly called an alibi is:**
(A) "He struck me first."
(B) "I didn't intend to hurt him."
(C) "I was miles away from there at the time."
(D) "I don't remember what happened."

12.   A person who, after the commission of a crime, conceals the offender with the intent that the latter may escape from arrest and trial, is called:
(A) an accessory   (B) an accomplice
(C) a confederate   (D) an associate.

13.   A sworn statement of fact is called:
(A) an affidavit   (B) an oath
(C) an acknowledgment (D) a subponea.

14. Among the following, the signature cards of a bank might be employed as a means of verifying an individual's
(A) character   (B) identity
(C) financial status (D) employment.

15. An accomplice is
(A) one, who after full knowledge that a felony has been committed, conceals same from the officers
(B) one who is liable to prosecution for the same identical offense charged against the defendant on trial
(C) one who harbors a person charged with or convicted of a felony
(D) a person who has knowledge of a given act.

END OF TEST

*Go on to do the following Test in this Examination, just as you would
be expected to do on the actual exam.*

TEST II. JUDGMENT AND REASONING

DIRECTIONS: For each question read all the choices care-fully. Then select that answer which you consider correct or most nearly correct. Blacken the answer space corresponding to your best choice, just as you would do on the actual examination.

In answering questions 1 and 2, make use of the following statement: "A description of persons or property wanted by this department which is to be given to the police force through the medium of a general alarm, if not distinctive, is of no value."

1. You are watching a great number of people leave a ball game. Of the persons who are described below the one whom it would be easiest to spot would be:
    (A) female; age 15; height 5'6"; weight 130 lbs.; long straight black hair
    (B) female; age 35; height 5'4"; weight 150 lbs.; wears glasses
    (C) male; age 60; height 5'7"; weight 170 lbs.; all false teeth
    (D) male; age 25; height 6'3"; weight 220 lbs.; pockmarked.

2. You are preparing the description of a woman to be broadcast. Of the following characteristics, the one which would be of most value to the driver of a squad car is:
    (A) frequents movie theatres
    (B) age 45 years
    (C) height 6'1"
    (D) smokes very heavily.

3. Under the portrait parle system of identification, of the following the most important part of a description of a person is the
    (A) dress, since it is the most noticeable
    (B) ears, since no two are alike
    (C) eyes, since they cannot be altered
    (D) nose, since it is most distinctive.

4. Assume that on a hot summer day you are stationed on the grass at the south bank of a busy parkway looking at eastbound traffic for a light blue Ford two-door sedan. If traffic is very heavy, the one of the following additional pieces of information which would be most helpful to you in identifying the car is that
    (A) all chrome is missing from the left side of the car

    (B) there is a bullet hole in the left front window
    (C) the paint on the right side of the car is somewhat faded
    (D) the front bumper is missing.

5. Assume that you have stopped a Dodge four-door sedan which you suspect is a car which has been reported as stolen the day before. The one of the following items of information which would be of greatest value in determining whether this is the stolen car is that
    (A) the stolen car's license number was QA 2356; this car's license number is U 21375
    (B) the stolen car's engine number was AB 6231; this car's engine number is CS 2315
    (C) the windshield of the stolen car was not cracked; this car's windshield is cracked
    (D) the stolen car had no dents; this car has numerous dents.

6. You are watching a great number of people leave a sports arena after a boxing match. Of the characteristics listed below, the one which would be of greatest value to you in spotting a man wanted by the Department is
    (A) Height: 5'3"; Weight: 200 lbs.
    (B) Eyes: brown; Hair: black, wavy; Complexion: sallow
    (C) Mustache: when last seen in August, he wore a small black mustache
    (D) Scars: thin ½" scar on left upper lip; Tattoos: on right forearm — "Pinto".

7. The only personal description the police have of a particular criminal was made several years ago. Of the following the item in the description that will be most useful in identifying him at the present time is the
    (A) color of his eyes
    (B) color of his hair
    (C) number of teeth
    (D) weight.

8. "Photographs of suspected persons should not be shown to a witness if the criminal himself can be arrested and placed on view for identification." The above recommendation is
(A) inadvisable; this procedure might subject the witness to future retribution by suspect
(B) advisable; a photograph cannot be used for identification purposes with the same degree of certainty as the suspect in person
(C) inadvisable; the appearance of the suspect may have changed since the commission of the crime
(D) advisable; photography as an art has not achieved an acceptable degree of perfection.

9. Stationed at a busy highway, you are given the description of a vehicle which has been stolen. Of the following characteristics, the one which will permit you to eliminate most easily a large number of vehicles is
(A) no spare tire
(B) make—Buick, two-door sedan
(C) color — black
(D) tires 750 x 16, white walled.

10. If a sick or injured woman, to whom a male trooper is rendering aid, is unknown and the trooper has reason to believe that her clothing contains a means of identification, the trooper should
(A) immediately search the clothing for such identification and remove any identification found therein
(B) send for a female trooper to search the clothing before the woman is sent to a hospital
(C) ask any female present to search the clothing for such identification
(D) accompany her to the hospital and there seek the necessary information from hospital authorities.

11. Which of the following means of avoiding identification would be most likely to meet with success?
(A) growing a beard
(B) shaving off the beard if there was one originally
(C) burning the fingers so as to remove the fingerprints
(D) changing the features by facial surgery.

12. In asking a witness to a crime to identify a suspect, it is a common practice to place the suspect with a group of persons and ask the witness to pick out the person in question. Of the following, the best reason for this practice is that it will
(A) make the identification more reliable than if the witness were shown the suspect alone
(B) protect the witness against reprisals
(C) make sure that the witness is telling the truth
(D) help select other participants in the crime at the same time.

13. "Social security cards are not acceptable proof of identification for police purposes." Of the following, the most important reason for this rule is that the social security card
(A) is easily obtained
(B) states on its face "for social security purposes—not for identification"
(C) is frequently lost
(D) does not contain a photograph, description or fingerprints of the person.

14. Of the following facts about a criminal the one which would be of most value in apprehending and identifying the criminal would be that he
(A) drives a black Chevrolet sedan with chrome license-plate holders
(B) invariably uses a .38 caliber Colt blue-steel revolver with walnut stock and regulation front sight
(C) talks with a French accent and frequently stutters
(D) usually wears 3-button single-breasted "Ivy League" suits and white oxford cloth button-down-collar shirts.

15. The investigator is tracing a fugitive suspect. Which of the following means of identification is the suspect least able to suppress?
(A) He suffers from chorea
(B) His picture is available for identification
(C) He is an habitual frequenter of a certain type of restaurant
(D) He is a rabid baseball fan.

END OF TEST

Go on to the next test in the examination, just as you would do on the actual exam. Check your answers when you have completed the entire examination. The answer key for this test, and all the other tests, will be found at the conclusion of this section.

TEST III. JUDGMENT AND REASONING

DIRECTIONS: Each of the following statements is either True or False. Mark the corresponding number on your answer sheet T if the statement is True, and F if the statement is False.

The answer key for this test will be found after the last test in this section.

1. In case of conflicting orders from two superior officers of the same rank, a State Trooper should always act on the last order given.

2. When a departmental regulation is particularly drastic, it is sometimes necessary for a State Trooper to use his or her better judgment and not enforce it.

3. **The best policy for a State Trooper to follow is to treat all violators of the law identically.**

4. When a motorist whom you have apprehended speeding, becomes abusive or insulting in language, it is best to answer in like manner.

5. **Imprisonment prevents the normal expression of many basic human wants.**

6. The success or failure of a State Trooper in handling people, depends, in large part, on intelligence and personality.

7. **An alienist is one who is empowered to grant rights of United States citizenship to foreigners.**

8. **Prevention of crimes is of greater value to the community than the punishment of criminals.**

9. **It is best procedure for a State Trooper never to listen to com -plaints of motorists.**

10. **It is improper for a State Trooper to accept a gratuity from an organization having business relations with his department under any and all circumstances.**

11. A prisoner in lawful custody under a charge of a felony, who escapes from custody, is guilty of a misdemeanor charge upon recapture.

12. It is better to use sand than water in putting out an oil fire.

13. An attempt to break out of a state prison is punishable as a felony.

14. A recidivist is one who tends to relapse into former criminal ways after punishment.

15. Emotionally unstable criminals require more severe discipline than others.

16. The process of returning a non-citizen of the United States to the country from which he came is known as extradition.

17. A State Trooper should use personal judgment in all cases involving questions of discipline.

18. Psychiatric examination of the prisoner is relatively an unimportant factor in modern penal treatment of prison inmates.

19. A minimum sentence must be served before any prisoner may be eligible for parole.

20. It is generally permissible for a State Trooper to unbutton his coat and tilt his hat when the weather is exceptionally hot.

21. It is difficult and dangerous to generalize as to an 'average' or 'typical' criminal.

22. To apprehend a criminal is to arrest and hold the person on a criminal charge with a view to trial.

23. It is generally a useless attempt to try to educate habitual speeders.

24. If a person is accused of arson, it means that the person is guilty of assault and battery.

25. Violations of the law can most effectively be halted by sentencing criminals to long prison terms at hard labor.

26. An assemblage of three persons is sufficient to cause a riot.

27. The State Trooper must take the attitude that the rules of the department must be followed, though they may seem somewhat strict in certain circumstances.

28. **Prisoners given indeterminate sentences are given time off for good behavior and conduct.**

29. **A traffic infraction under the traffic law may not properly be called a crime.**

30. **Suffocation is a condition where consciousness is partially or completely lost because of defective oxidation of the blood.**

31. **An indeterminate sentence generally has a prescribed minimum and maximum limit.**

END OF TEST

Go on to the next test in the examination, just as you would do on the actual exam. Check your answers when you have completed the entire examination.

TEST IV. JUDGMENT AND REASONING

DIRECTIONS: Each of the following statements is either True or False. Mark the corresponding number on your answer sheet T if the statement is True, and F if the statement is False.

The answer key for this test will be found after the last test in this section.

1. **The action of an 'accessory' to a felony generally is one occurring when the crime has already been committed.**
2. A State Trooper may inflict any punishment upon a prisoner for disobediency.
3. **The correctional institution should properly be thought of as an educational institution.**
4. The reformation of the criminal is relatively unimportant as contrasted with the objective of keeping the criminal securely confined.
5. **A State Trooper may not generally be punished for accepting a small bribe.**
6. **It is good policy to order motorists about because they will then be impressed by your attitude and authority.**
7. **Knowingly harboring a criminal after commission of a crime is not necessarily a criminal offense.**
8. **A crime is either a felony or a misdemeanor.**
9. A public police officer, convicted of a crime, must forfeit the office.
10. **The sole function of a prison is to provide a place of detention for persons who have been convicted of crime.**
11. It is the duty of a trooper to go to the immediate assistance of a fellow trooper who is in trouble.
12. A State Trooper who through negligence in duties permits a prisoner to escape, is not open to a criminal charge.
13. **It is unlawful for a civilian to interfere with a prisoner working on the public highway.**
14. **Blackmail has to do with a violation of the public peace as by an act of violence.**
15. **One of the factors in abnormal prison behavior is the effect of prison isolation and restriction.**
16. **Alertness and the ability to do the right thing at the right time are vital elements in the equipment of the State Trooper.**

17. An alias is a term used in legal phraseology in connection with names assumed with questionable motives for concealment.

18. **An alibi is a defense in which it is usually claimed that the defendant was at the scene of the crime at the time it was committed.**

19. **Most prison inmates are illiterate.**

20. **Inequalities in the administration of justice set up antagonisms in the minds of criminals against the law, society and the institution.**

21. **Insufficient and unwholesome foods tend toward provoking prison riots.**

22. **A "stretch" refers to a term of imprisonment in prison language.**

23. **Penology does not mean the same as criminology.**

24. **In police work, intelligence and personality must take precedence over mere physical size and brute force.**

25. **The primary objectives of imprisonment are security and punishment.**

26. **The disproportionate number of Blacks among the prison population is an indication that the Black is inherently lawless.**

27. The State Trooper should never borrow money because it will lead to evil habits.

28. **It is not a good policy for a State Trooper to give a motorist due credit for being intelligent.**

29. **A State Trooper should never be permitted to read or write while on duty.**

30. **In an emergency, there is seldom time for explanations by superior officers.**

END OF TEST

Go on to the next test in the examination, just as you would do on the actual exam. Check your answers when you have completed the entire examination.

TEST V. READING COMPREHENSION AND INTERPRETATION

DIRECTIONS: Below each of the following passages, you will find questions or incomplete statements about the passage. Each statement or question is followed by lettered words or expressions. Select the word or expression that most satisfactorily completes each statement or answers each question in accordance with the meaning of the passage.

Questions 1 and 2 pertain to the following section of the Penal Code:

"Section 1942. A person who, after having been three times convicted within this state, of felonies or attempts to commit felonies, or under the law of any other state, government or country, of crimes which if committed within this state would be felonious, commits a felony, other than murder, first or second degree, or treason, within this state, shall be sentenced upon conviction of such fourth, or subsequent, offense to imprisonment in a state prison for an indeterminate term the minimum of which shall be not less than the maximum term provided for first offenders for the crime for which the individual has been convicted, but, in any event, the minimum term upon conviction for a felony as the fourth or subsequent, offense, shall be not less than fifteen years, and the maximum thereof shall be his natural life."

1. Under the terms of the above quoted portion of Section 1942 of the Penal Law, a person must receive the increased punishment therein provided, if
   (A) convicted of a felony and three times previously convicted of felonies
   (B) three times previously convicted of felonies, regardless of the nature of the present conviction
   (C) the fourth conviction is for murder, first or second degree, or treason
   (D) previously convicted three times of murder, first or second degree, or treason.

2. Under the terms of the above quoted portion of Section 1942 of the Penal Law, a person convicted of a felony for which the penalty is imprisonment for a term not to exceed ten years, and who has been three times previously convicted of felonies in this state, shall be sentenced to a term the minimum of which shall be
   (A) ten years

   (B) fifteen years
   (C) indeterminate
   (D) his natural life.

Answer questions 3 to 6 on the basis of the following statement:

Disorderly conduct, in the abstract, does not constitute any crime known to law; it is only when it tends to be a breach of the peace under the circumstances detailed in section 1458 of the Consolidation Act, that it constitutes a minor offense cognizable by the Justice of the Criminal Court, and when it in fact threatens to disturb the peace it is a misdemeanor as well under section 675 of the Penal Code as at common law, and not within the jurisdiction of the judge, but of the Criminal Court.

3. Of the following, the most accurate statement on the basis of this paragraph is that
   (A) an act which merely threatens to disturb the peace is not a crime
   (B) disorderly conduct, by itself, is not a crime
   (C) some types of disorderly conduct are indictable
   (D) a minor offense may or may not be cognizable by the police.

4. Of the following, the least accurate statement on the basis of the preceding paragraph is that
   (A) disorderly conduct which threatens to disturb the peace is within the jurisdiction of a judge
   (B) disorderly conduct which "tends to be a breach of peace" may constitute a minor offense
   (C) section 1458 of the Consolidation Act discusses a "breach of the peace"

(D) disorderly conduct which "tends to be a breach of the peace" is not the same as that which threatens to disturb the peace.

5. The paragraph distinguishes least sharply between

(A) the Penal Code and the Common Law
(B) disorderly conduct as a crime and disorderly conduct as no crime
(C) what "tends to be a breach of peace" and what threatens to disturb the peace
(D) a minor offense and a misdemeanor.

6. Of the following generalizations, the one which is best illustrated by the paragraph is that

(A) acts which in themselves are not criminal may become criminal as a result of their effect
(B) abstract conduct may, in and of itself, be criminal
(C) criminal acts are determined by results rather than by intent
(D) an act which is criminal to begin with may not be criminal if it fails to have the desired effect.

Answer questions 7 and 8 solely on the basis of the following paragraph:

"If a motor vehicle fails to pass inspection, the owner will be given a rejection notice by the inspection station. Repairs must be made within ten days after this notice is issued. It is not necessary to have the required adjustment or repairs made at the station where the inspection occurred. The vehicle may be taken to any other garage. Re-inspection after repairs may be made at any official inspection station, not necessarily the same station which made the initial inspection. The registration of any motor vehicle for which an inspection sticker has not been obtained as required, or which is not repaired and inspected within ten days after inspection indicates defects, is subject to suspension. A vehicle cannot be used on public highways while its registration is under suspension."

7. According to this paragraph, the owner of a car which does not pass inspection must

(A) have repairs made at the same station which rejected the car
(B) take the car to another station and have it re-inspected

(C) have repairs made anywhere and then have the car re-inspected
(D) not use the car on a public highway until the necessary repairs have been made.

8. According to the paragraph, the one of the following which may be cause for suspension of the registration of a vehicle is that

(A) an inspection sticker was issued before the rejection notice had been in force for ten days
(B) it was not re-inspected by the station that rejected it originally
(C) it was not re-inspected either by the station that rejected it originally or by the garage which made the repairs
(D) it has not had defective parts repaired within ten days after inspection.

9. A statute states: "A person who steals an article worth less than $100 where no aggravating circumstances accompany the act, is guilty of petit larceny. If the article is worth $100 or more it may be larceny second degree." If all you know is that Edward Smith stole an article worth $100, it may reasonably be said that

(A) Smith is guilty of petit larceny
(B) Smith is guilty of larceny second degree
(C) Smith is guilty of neither petit larceny nor larceny second degree
(D) precisely what charge will be placed against Smith is uncertain.

10. An ordinance reads: "All vehicles, such as motorcycles, passenger automobiles, automobile trucks, horsedriven wagons, or any other type of conveyance, are prohibited from using any street designated as a play street, except as the requirements of the residents of the property abutting such play street may call for." John White, who had only recently arrived in the city from Montreal, Canada, where he had lived all of his life, was given a summons by Officer Kelly for violating this ordinance. At the time he received the summons he was delivering groceries to a resident on the play street for the Smith Grocery Company, for whom he had started to work the day before. There were no children playing in the street at the time and he did not know that it was a play street. Officer Kelly should be told that the summons should not have been issued because

(A) there were no children on the street at the time
(B) he was delivering groceries to a resident on the street

(C) not being a citizen of the United States, he is not completely subject to our jurisdiction

(D) he did not know that it was a play street.

11. "A 'felony' is a crime punishable by death or imprisonment in a state prison, and any other crime is a 'misdemeanor.'" According to this quotation the decisive distinction between "felony" and "misdemeanor" is the
(A) degree of criminality
(B) type of crime
(C) place of incarceration
(D) length of imprisonment.

Answer questions 12 to 15 on the basis of the following statement:

"The question, whether an act, repugnant to the Constitution, can become the law of the land, is a question deeply interesting to the United States; but, happily, not of an intricacy proportioned to its interest. It seems only necessary to recognize certain principles, supposed to have been long and well established, to decide it. That the people have an original right to establish, for their future government, such principles as, in their opinion, shall most conduce to their own happiness, is the basis on which the whole American fabric has been erected. The exercise of this original right is a very great exertion; nor can it, nor ought it, to be frequently repeated. The principles, therefore, so established, are deemed fundamental: and as the authority from which they proceed is supreme, and can seldom act, they are designed to be permanent."

12. The best title for this paragraph would be
(A) Principles of the Constitution
(B) The Root of Constitutional Change
(C) Only People Can Change the Constitution

(D) Methods of Constitutional Change.

13. According to this paragraph, original right is
(A) fundamental to the principle that the people may choose their own form of government
(B) established by the Constitution
(C) the result of a very great exertion and should not often be repeated
(D) supreme, can seldom act, and is designed to be permanent.

14. Whether a fact not in keeping with Constitutional principles can become a law is, according to the paragraph

(A) an intricate problem requiring great thought and concentration
(B) determined by the proportionate interests of legislators
(C) an intricate problem, but less intricate than it would seem from the interest shown in it
(D) determined by certain long established principles, fundamental to Constitutional law.

15. According to the paragraph, the phrase, "and can seldom act," refers to

(A) the principles early enacted into law by Americans when they chose their future form of government
(B) the original rights of the people as vested in the Constitution
(C) the body of laws by which the life and actions of all people are governed
(D) the established, fundamental principles of government.

END OF TEST

*Go on to do the following Test in this Examination, just as you would
be expected to do on the actual exam.*

TEST VI. READING COMPREHENSION AND INTERPRETATION

DIRECTIONS: This test consists of several reading passages, each followed by a number of statements. Analyze each statement solely on the basis of the material given. Then, mark your answer sheet (A) (B) (C) or (D).
Mark it (A) if the statement is entirely true.
Mark it (B) if the statement is entirely false
Mark it (C) if the statement is partially false and partially true.
Mark it (D) if the statement cannot be judged on the basis of the facts given in the excerpt.

READING PASSAGE

"The Commissioner of Correction may permit any prisoner confined in a state prison, excepting one awaiting the sentence of death, to attend the funeral of his or her father, mother, child, brother, sister, husband or wife, within the state, or to visit such relative during his or her illness if death is imminent. Any expenses incurred under these provisions, with respect to any prisoner, shall be deemed an expense of maintenance of the prison and be paid from moneys available therefor; but the warden, if the rules and regulations of the Commissioner of Correction shall so provide, may allow the prisoner or any one in his behalf, to reimburse the state for such expense."

1. If a near relative is on the point of death, a state prisoner is generally permitted to leave the prison for a visit.

2. The travelling expenses of a state prisoner who attends the funeral of a relative are paid for either by the prisoner or the warden.

3. The only circumstances under which a state prisoner is granted permission to leave the prison is in the event of a funeral for a near relative.

4. Under no circumstances is a state prisoner forbidden to attend the funeral of his wife, provided it takes place within the state.

5. Under no circumstances is a state prisoner ever permitted out of the state to attend the funeral of a close relative.

READING PASSAGE

"The Board of Parole is charged with the duty of determining which prisoners, serving an indeterminate sentence in either the state prisons or the Elmira Reformatory, are subject to release on parole, when, and under what conditions. The Board also has the responsibility for supervising all prisoners released on parole from state prisons, for making such investigations as may be necessary in connection therewith, and for determining whether violation of parole conditions exist in specific cases. The Board must make a personal study of the prisoners confined in the prisons under indeterminate sentence, in order to determine their fitness for parole."

6. Only prisoners in state prisons are subject to parole.

7. An indeterminate sentence can be likened to an indefinite sentence.

8. Only prisoners serving indeterminate sentences may be considered for parole.

9. The Board of Parole has jurisdiction over prospective parolees.

10. Although the Board of Parole has the responsibility for supervising paroled prisoners, their fitness for parole is determined by an impersonal study of the prisoners.

READING PASSAGE

"Every person sentenced to an indeterminate sentence and confined to a state prison when the person has served a period of time equal to the minimum sentence imposed by the court for the crime for which he or she was convicted, is subject to the jurisdiction of the Board of Parole. The time of release is within the discretion of the Board, but no such person may be released until he or she has served such minimum sentence nor until he or she has served one year. The action of the Board in releasing prisoners is deemed a judicial function, and is not reviewable if done according to law. No person may be released on parole merely as a reward for good conduct or efficient performance of duties assigned in prison, but only if the Board of Parole is of the opinion that there is reasonable probability that, if such prisoner is released, he or she will live and remain at liberty without violating the law, and that the release is not incompatible with the welfare of society."

11. A paroled prisoner generally remains in the legal custody of the prison from which he or she was paroled.

12. When the Board of Parole releases a prisoner on parole, the Board's power is like that of a judge and may not be reviewed if lawful.

13. Prisoners under an indeterminate sentence are subject to the jurisdiction of the Board of Parole, but only when they have served their maximum sentence.

14. Prisoners are generally paroled on the basis of good conduct entirely.

15. No prisoner may be paroled without having served a minimum of a year in any case.

READING PASSAGE

"A sentence of imprisonment in a state prison for a definite fixed period of time is a definite sentence. A sentence to imprisonment in a state prison, having minimum and maximum limits fixed by the court or the governor, is an indeterminate sentence. Every prisoner confined to a state prison or penitentiary may, in the discretion of the governor, receive, for good conduct and efficient and willing performance of duties assigned, a reduction of sentence not to exceed ten days for each month of the minimum term in the case of an indeterminate sentence, or of the term as imposed by the court in the case of a definite sentence. The maximum reduction allowable under this provision shall be four months per year, but nothing herein contained shall be construed to confer any right whatsoever upon any prisoner to demand or require the whole or any part of such reduction."

16. Only prisoners under indeterminate sentence are subject to parole.

17. Prisoners given indeterminate sentences are allowed time off for good behavior and conduct which is not the case with prisoners under definite sentence.

18. A definite sentence generally has prescribed minimum and maximum limits.

19. Under the law, all prisoners must receive time off their sentence for good conduct and efficient and willing performance of duties assigned.

20. The maximum limit of an indeterminate sentence may be set by the governor or the judge of the court in which sentence is imposed.

END OF TEST

Go on to the next test in the examination, just as you would do on the actual exam. Check your answers when you have completed the entire examination.

TEST VII. ARITHMETIC COMPUTATIONS

DIRECTIONS: Each problem in this test involves a certain amount of logical reasoning and thinking on your part, besides the usual simple computations, to help you in finding the solution. Read each problem carefully and choose the correct answer from the four choices that follow. When you have finished, check your answers with the answer key at the end of the test.

1. If the average cost of sweeping a square foot of a city street is $7.50, the cost of sweeping 100 square feet is

    (A) $75.00
    (C) $750.00
    (B) $7,500.00
    (D) $700.00

2. If a Sanitation Department scow is towed at the rate of three miles an hour it will need how many hours to go 28 miles?

    (A)   10 hrs. 30 min.   (B)   12 hrs.
    (C)   9 hrs. 20 min.   (D)   9 hrs. 15 min.

3. If a truck is 60 feet away from a sanitation worker, it is how many feet nearer to him than a truck which is 100 feet away?

    (A)   60 ft.   (B)   40 ft.
    (C)   50 ft.   (D)   20 ft.

4. A clerk divided his 35 hour work week as follows: 1/5 of his time in sorting mail; ½ of his time in filing letters; and 1/7 of his time in reception work. The rest of his time was devoted to messenger work. The percentage of time spent on messenger work by the clerk during the week was most nearly

    (A) 6%   (B) 10%
    (C) 14%   (D) 16%

5. Twelve clerks are assigned to enter certain data on index cards. This number of clerks could perform the task in 18 days. After these clerks have worked on this assignment for 6 days, 4 more clerks are added to the staff to do this work. Assuming that all the clerks work at the same rate of speed, the entire task, instead of taking 18 days, will be performed in

    (A) 9 days   (B) 12 days
    (C) 17 days   (D) 15 days

6. Six gross of special drawing pencils were purchased for use in a city department. If the pencils were used at the rate of 24 a week, the maximum number of weeks that the six gross of pencils would last is

    (A)   6 weeks   (B)   12 weeks
    (C)   24 weeks   (D)   36 weeks

7. A man worked 30 days. He paid 2/5 of his earnings for board and room and had $720 left. What was his daily wage?

    (A) $47.50
    (C) $55.00
    (B) $40.00
    (D) $42.50

8. After gaining 50% of his original capital, a man had a capital of $18,000. Find the original capital.

    (A) $12,200.00   (B) $13,100.00
    (C) $12,000.00   (D) $12,025.00

9. A cog wheel having 8 cogs plays into another cog wheel having 24 cogs. When the small wheel has made 42 revolutions, how many has the larger wheel made?

    (A) 14   (B) 20
    (C) 16   (D) 10

10. A dealer bought some motorcycles for $4000. He sold them for $6200, making $50 on each motorcycle. How many motorcycles were there?

    (A) 40   (B) 38
    (C) 43   (D) 44

11. A firm had ¼ of its capital invested in goods, ⅔ of the remainder in land, and the remainder, $1224, in cash. What was the capital of the firm?

    (A) $4,986.00   (B) $4,698.00
    (C) $4,896.00   (D) $4,869.00

12. A and B together earn $2100. If B is paid ¼ more than A, how many dollars should B receive?

    (A) $1,166.66⅔   (B) $1,161.66⅔
    (C) $1,616.66⅓   (D) $1,166.66⅓

13. If a house is bought for $21,500 and sold again for $23,650, what is the gain per cent?

    (A) 8%   (B) 15%
    (C) 20%   (D) 10%

14. A person owned 5/6 of a piece of property and sold ¾ of his share for $1800. What was the value of the property?

    (A) $2,808.00   (B) $2,880.00
    (C) $2,088.00   (D) $2,880.80

END OF EXAMINATION

If you finish before the allotted time is up, check your work. When time runs out, compare your answers for this test and all the other tests in the examination with the answer key that follows.

ANSWER KEY FOR FINAL SAMPLE PRACTICE EXAMINATION

TEST I. JUDGMENT AND REASONING

1.C	4.A	7.C	10.B	13.A
2.C	5.D	8.D	11.C	14.B
3.A	6.A	9.B	12.A	15.A

TEST II. JUDGMENT AND REASONING

1.D	4.D	7.A	10.D	13.C
2.C	5.B	8.B	11.D	14.C
3.B	6.A	9.B	12.A	15.A

TEST III. JUDGMENT AND REASONING

1.F	5.T	9.F	13.T	17.F	21.T	25.F	29.T
2.F	6.T	10.T	14.T	18.F	22.T	26.T	30.T
3.F	7.F	11.F	15.F	19.T	23.F	27.T	31.T
4.F	8.T	12.T	16.F	20.F	24.F	28.T	

TEST IV. JUDGMENT AND REASONING

1.F	5.F	9.T	13.T	17.T	21.T	25.F	28.F
2.F	6.F	10.F	14.F	18.F	22.T	26.F	29.F
3.T	7.F	11.T	15.T	19.F	23.T	27.F	30.F
4.F	8.T	12.F	16.T	20.T	24.T		

TEST V. READING COMPREHENSION AND INTERPRETATION

1.A	4.A	7.C	10.B	13.A
2.B	5.E	8.D	11.C	14.C
3.B	6.A	9.D	12.B	15.A

TEST VI. READING COMPREHENSION AND INTERPRETATION

1.A	4.B	7.D	10.C	13.C	16.D	19.B
2.C	5.D	8.D	11.D	14.B	17.C	20.A
3.B	6.B	9.A	12.A	15.A	18.B	

TEST VII. ARITHMETIC COMPUTATIONS

1.C	4.D	7.B	10.D	13.D
2.C	5.D	8.C	11.C	14.B
3.B	6.D	9.A	12.A	

MORE ARCO BOOKS

Perhaps you've discovered that you are weak in language, verbal ability or mathematics. Why flounder and fail when help is so easily available? Brush up in the privacy of your own home with one of our review books.

At the same time, choose from our wide range of hobby and general interest books, designed to entertain and inform you in whatever area you select.

Each of the following books was created under the same expert editorial supervision that produced the excellent book you are now using. Whatever your goals or interests...you can learn more and score higher on tests with Arco.

CIVIL SERVICE AND TEST PREPARATION—GENERAL

MILITARY EXAMINATION SERIES

HIGH SCHOOL AND COLLEGE PREPARATION

Scholastic Aptitude Tests 04920-0 6.95
Scoring High On College Entrance Tests 01858-5 5.00
Scoring High On Reading Tests 00731-1 5.00
Student's Career Guide to a Future in the Allied
   Health Professions, Ilk 04921-9 6.95
Test of Standard Written English (TSWE),
   Arco Editorial Board 04748-8 3.95
Total Math Review for the GMAT, GRE and Other Graduate
   School Admission Tests, Frieder 04981-2 8.00
Triple Your Reading Speed, Cutler 02083-0 5.00
Typing for Everyone, Levine 04975-8 6.95
Verbal Workbook for the SAT,
   Freedman & Haller 04853-0 6.00

GED PREPARATION

Basic Mathematics, Castellano & Seitz 05126-4 5.00
Basic Skills in Writing, Kindilien 05264-3 4.95
Comprehensive Math Review for the High School
   Equivalency Diploma Test, McDonough 03420-3 4.00
New High School Equivalency Diploma Tests 04451-9 5.95
Preliminary Arithmetic for the High School Equivalency
   Diploma Test 02165-9 5.00
Preliminary Practice for the High School Equivalency
   Diploma Test 01441-5 6.00
Preparation for the Spanish High School Equivalency
   Diploma (Preparaction Para El Examen De Equivalencia
   De La Escuela Superior—En Espanol),
   Lanzano, Abreu, Ringel, Banks & Sagrista 05095-0 6.95
Step-By-Step Guide to Correct English, Pulaski 03402-5 3.95

General Education Development Series

Correctness and Effectiveness of Expression (English HSEDT),
   Castellano, Guercio & Seitz 03688-5 4.00
General Mathematical Ability (Mathematics HSEDT),
   Castellano, Guercio & Seitz 03689-3 6.00
Reading Interpretation in Social Sciences, Natural Sciences,
   and Literature (Reading HSEDT), Castellano,
   Guercio & Seitz 03690-7 5.00
Teacher's Manual for GED Series, Castellano
   Guercio, & Seitz 03692-3 2.50

COLLEGE BOARD ACHIEVEMENT TESTS/CBAT

American History and Social Studies Achievement Test—
   Second Edition 04337-7 5.95
Biology Achievement Test—Second Edition,
   Solomon & Spector 04094-7 3.95
Chemistry Achievement Test 04101-3 3.95
English Composition Achievement Test 04338-5 5.95
German Achievement Test, Greiner 01698-1 1.45
Mathematics: Level I Achievement Test, Bramson 05319-4 3.00
CBAT Mathematics Level II, Bramson 04284-2 4.95
Spanish Achievement Test, Jassey 01741-4 1.45

ARCO COLLEGE OUTLINES

American History to 1877 .... 04726-7 3.95
American History from 1877 .... 04730-5 3.95
World History Part I 04729-1 3.95
World History Part II 04731-3 3.95

ARCO SCHOLARSHIP EXAMINATION SERIES

AP

Advanced Placement Music, Seligson-Ross 04743-7 4.95

AP/CBAT

Advanced Placement and College Board
   Achievement Tests in Physics (B-C),
   Arco Editorial Board 04493-4 6.95

AP/CLEP

Advanced Placement and College Level Examinations in
   American History, Woloch 03804-7 5.95
Advanced Placement and College Level Examinations in
   Biology, Arco Editorial Board 04415-2 5.95
Advanced Placement and College Level Examinations in
   Chemistry 04484-5 4.95
Advanced Placement and College Level Examinations in
   English—Analysis and Interpretation of Literature .. 04406-3 4.95

AP/CLEP/CBAT

Advanced Placement, College Level Examinations and
   College Board Achievement Tests In European
   History 04407-1 5.95

CLEP

College Level Examination in Composition and Freshman
   English 03798-9 4.95

College Level Examination Program 04150-1 6.00

College Level Examination Program:
   The General Examination in the Humanities 04727-5 6.95

College Level Examinations in Mathematics: College
   Algebra, College Algebra-Trigonometry,
   Trigonometry 04339-3 5.95

MEDICINE

MEDICAL REVIEW BOOKS

Basic Dental Sciences Review, DeMarco 03396-7 10.00
Basic Science Nursing Review, Cheatham,
   Fitzsimmons, Lessner, King, Lafferty,
   DePace & Blumenstein 05133-7 8.00
Biochemistry Review, Silverman 04359-8 12.00
Clinical Dental Sciences Review, DeMarco 03383-5 10.00
Comprehensive Medical Boards Examination Review,
   second revised edition, Horemis 01595-0 8.00
Dental Assistants Examination Review, Hirsch 03902-7 9.00
Dental Hygiene Examination Review, Armstrong 04283-4 10.00

Endocrinology Review, Hsu 04228-1 12.00
General Pathology Review, Lewis & Kerwin 04774-7 10.00
Histology and Embryology Review, Amenta 03831-4 8.00
Human Anatomy Review, Montgomery & Singleton 03368-1 8.00
Human Physiology Examination Review, Shepard 04826-3 12.00
Internal Medicine Review, Pieroni 03881-0 11.00
Medical Assistants Examination Review, second edition,
   Clement 04854-9 10.00
Medical Examinations: A Preparation Guide, Bhardwaj .. 03944-2 9.00
Medical Technology Examination Review, Hossaini 04365-2 10.00
Microbiology and Immunology Review, Second edition,
   Rothfield, Ward & Tilton 04882-4 10.00

Neuroscience and Clinical Neurology Review, Goldblatt . 03370-3 **10.00**
Nuclear Medicine Technology
    Examination Review, Spies 04724-0 **12.00**
Obstretrics and Gynecology Review, Second edition,
    Vontver 03450-5 **9.00**
Patient Management Problems:
    Obstetrics and Gynecology, DeCherney 04364-4 **8.00**
Patient Management Problems:
    Pediatrics, Howell & Simon 04780-1 **10.00**
Patient Management Problems: Surgery, Rosenberg ... 04654-6 **8.00**
Pediatrics Review, Second edition, Lorin 03375-4 **8.00**
Pharmacology Review, Ellis...................... 04108-0 **10.00**
Pharmacy Review, Second edition, Singer........... 04878-6 **12.00**
Physical Medicine and Rehabilitation
    Review, Schuchmann 04723-2 **15.00**
Physician's Assistant Examination Review,
    Aschenbrener 04026-2 **12.00**
Psychiatry Examination Review—Second Edition,
    Easson 03395-9 **8.00**
Psychiatry: Patient Management Review, Easson 04058-0 **8.00**
Public Health and Preventive Medicine Review 04690-2 **9.00**
Pulmonary Disease Review, Hall 04008-4 **12.00**
Radiologic Technology Examination Review,
    Naidech & Damon 03833-0 **8.00**
Specialty Board Review: Anatomic Pathology,
    Gravanis & Johnson 03858-6 **14.00**
Specialty Board Review: Anesthesiology, Beach 04112-9 **14.00**
Specialty Board Review: Family Practice,
    Bhardwaj & Yen 03943-4 **12.00**
Specialty Board Review: General Surgery,
    Rob & Hinshaw 03494-7 **12.00**
Specialty Board Review: Internal Medicine, Pieroni ... 04818-2 **14.00**
Specialty Board Review: Obstetrics and
    Gynecology, Williams 03477-7 **14.00**
Specialty Board Review: Psychiatry, Atkins........... 03471-8 **12.00**
Surgery Review, Kountz et al 03880-2 **8.00**
Systemic Pathology Review, Lewis & Kerwin 04930-8 **12.00**

MEDIBOOKS

Fundamentals of Radiation Therapy, Lowry 03462-9 **7.50**
Midwifery, Hallum.............................. 03460-2 **5.50**
Pathology, Mayers 04774-7 **6.00**

Principles of Intensive Care, Emery, Yates & Moorhead . 03461-0 **6.00**

MEDICAL TEXTBOOKS AND MANUALS

The Basis of Clinical Diagnosis, Parkins & Pegrum 03660-5 **12.95**
Differential Diagnosis in Gynecology,
    Vontver & Gamette 04129-3 **12.00**
Differential Diagnosis in Neurology, Smith........... 04033-5 **14.00**
Differential Diagnosis in Obstetrics, Williams
    & Joseph 04161-7 **10.00**
Differential Diagnosis in Disorders of the Eye,
    Kupfer & Kaiser-Kupfer 04315-6 **10.00**
Differential Diagnosis in Otolaryngology, Lee......... 04017-2 **14.00**
Differntial Diagnosis of Renal and Electrolyte Disorders,
    Klahr...................................... 04063-7 **14.00**
The Effective Scutboy, Harrell & Firestein 05159-0 **7.50**
Emergency Medicine, Hocutt 04983-9 **12.00**
Hospital-Based Education, Linton & Truelove 04776-3 **10.00**
Modern Medicine, Read et al...................... 04124-2 **14.75**
Psychiatry: A Concise Textbook for Primary
    Care Practitioners, Kraft et al 03924-8 **12.00**
Simplified Mathematics for Nurses,
    McElroy, Carr & Carr 04197-8 **5.00**

NURSING REVIEW BOOKS

Arco's Comprehensive State Board
    Examination Review for Nurses, Carter 04925-1 **8.95**
Child Health Nursing Review, Second edition, Porter ... 04825-5 **7.00**
Fundamentals of Nursing Review, Carter 04512-4 **6.00**
Maternal Health Nursing Review, Second edition,
    Sagebeer 04822-0 **6.00**
Medical-Surgical Nursing Examination Review,
    Second edition, Horemis & Matamors 02511-5 **6.00**
Medical-Surgical Nursing Review, Second edition,
    Hazzard.................................... 04823-9 **6.00**
Nursing Comprehensive Examination Review,
    second revised edition, Horemis 02499-2 **6.00**
Nursing Exam Review in Basic Sciences,
    Horemis & Matamors 02946-3 **4.00**
Practical Nursing Review, Second edition, Redempta ... 04827-1 **7.50**
Practice Tests for the L.P.N., Crow & Lounsbury....... 05189-2 **7.50**
Psychiatric/Mental Health Nursing Review,
    Second Edition, Rodgers & McGovern.............. 04824-7 **6.00**

PROFESSIONAL CAREER EXAM SERIES

Action Guide for Executive Job Seekers and Employers,
    Uris.. 01787-2 **3.95**
Air Traffic Controller, Morrison 04593-0 **10.00**
The Anatomy of Arson, French ....LR 04423-3 **12.50**
Arson: A Handbook of Detection and
    Investigation, Battle & Weston ....LR 04532-9 **9.95**
Automobile Mechanic Certification Tests, Sharp 03809-8 **6.00**
Bar Exams 01124-6 **5.00**
Careers for the Community College Graduate,
    Chernow & Chernow 05091-8 **5.95**
Certificate In Data Processing
    Examination, Morrison 04922-7 **12.00**
The C.P.A. Exam: Accounting by the "Parallel Point"
    Method, Lipscomb.........................LR 01103-3 **25.00**
Computer Programmer Analyst Trainee, Luftig 05310-0 **8.00**
Computers and Automation, Brown 01745-7 **5.95**
Computers and Data Processing Examinations:
    CDP/CCP/CLEP 04670-8 **10.00**
Dental Admission Test, Eighth ed.,
    Arco Editorial Board 05313-5 **6.00**
Graduate Management Admission Test 04914-6 **6.95**
Graduate Record Examination Aptitude Test 04910-3 **6.95**

Health Insurance Agent, Snouffer 04307-5 **8.00**
Health Profession Careers In Medicine's
    New Technology, Nassif 04436-5 **5.95**
How a Computer System Works, Brown & Workman 03424-6 **5.95**
How to Become a Successful Model—Second Edition,
    Krem......................................04508-6 **2.95**
How to Get into Medical and Dental School, revised
    edition, Shugar, Shugar, Bauman & Bauman 05112-4 **6.95**
How to Make Money in Music, Harris & Farrar 04089-0 **5.95**
How to Remember Anything, Markoff, Dubin & Carcel ...03929-9 **5.00**
How to Write Successful Business Letters,
    Riebel 02290-6 **5.00**
The Installation and Servicing of Domestic
    Oil Burners, Mitchell & Mitchell 00437-1 **10.00**
Instrument Pilot Examination, Morrison 04592-2 **9.95**
Law School Admission Test, Candrilli & Slawsky 05153-1 **6.95**
Life Insurance Agent, Snouffer 04306-7 **8.00**
Medicine's New Technology, Nassif................LR 04443-8 **9.95**
Miller Analogies Test 04990-1 **5.00**
Modern Police Service Encyclopedia, Salottolo 02389-9 **8.00**
National Career Directory, Gale & Gale 04510-8 **5.95**
The New Medical College Admission Test 04551-5 **6.95**

The Official 1981-82 Guide to Airline
  Careers, Morton 05238-4 7.95
The Official 1981-82 Guide to Steward
  and Stewardess Careers, Morton 05237-6 7.95
The Official 1981-82 Guide to Travel
  Agent and Travel Careers, Morton 05236-8 7.95
Notary Public 00180-1 6.00
Nursing School Entrance Examinations 01202-1 6.00
Playground and Recreation Director's Handbook 01096-7 8.00
Practice for U.S. Citizenship, Paz 05305-4 2.95
Preparacion para el Examen de la Licencia en Cosmetologia,
  McDonald & Mottram 05306-2 6.95
Preparation for Cosmetology Licensing
  Examination, McDonald & Mottram 04756-9 6.95
Preparation for Pesticide Certification
  Examinations, Frishman 04761-5 10.00
Principles of Data Processing, Morrison 04268-0 7.50
Property and Casualty Insurance
  Agent, Snouffer 04308-3 8.00
Psychology: A Graduate Review, Ozehosky & Polz 04136-6 10.00
The Real Estate Career Guide, Pivar 04790-9 7.95
Real Estate License Examinations, Martin 04794-1 8.00
Real Estate Mathematics Simplified, Shulman 04713-5 5.00
Refrigeration License Manual, Harfenist 02726-6 12.00
Resumes for Job Hunters, Shykind 03961-2 5.00
Resumes That Get Jobs, third edition,
  Resume Service 05210-4 3.95
Science Review for Medical College Admission,
  Morrison 04705-4 12.95
Simplify Legal Writing, Biskind 03801-2 5.00
Spanish for Nurses and Allied Health Science Students
  Hernandez-Miyares & Alba...................... 04127-7 10.00
Stationary Engineer and Fireman 00070-8 8.00
Structural Design 04549-3 10.00
Successful Public Speaking, Hull .... LR 02395-3 5.95
The Test of English as a Foreign
  Language (TOEFL), Moreno, Babin & Cordes......... 04450-0 8.95
TOEFL Listening Comprehension Cassette 04667-8 7.95
Travel Agent and Tourism, Morrison 04746-1 15.00
Veterinary College Admissions 04147-1 10.00
Your Job: Where to Find It—How to Get It, Corwen 05131-0 6.95
Your Resume—Key to a Better Job, Corwen 03733-4 4.00

ADVANCED GRE SERIES

Biology: Advanced Test for G.R.E., Solomon 04310-5 5.95
Business: Advanced Test for the G.R.E., Berman,
  Malea & Yearwood............................ 01599-3 4.95
Chemistry: Advanced Test for the G.R.E.,
  Weiss & Bozimo.............................. 01069-X 4.95
Economics: Advanced Test for the G.R.E.,
  Morrison 04548-5 5.95
Education: Advanced Test for the G.R.E.,
  Arco Editorial Board........................... 04714-3 6.95
French: Advanced Test for the G.R.E., Dethierry 01070-3 5.95
Geology: Advanced Test for the G.R.E., Dolgoff 01071-1 3.95
History: Advanced Test for the G.R.E.,
  Arco Editorial Board........................... 04414-4 5.95
Literature: Advanced Test for the G.R.E. 01073-8 3.95
Mathematics: Advanced Test for the G.R.E.,
  Bramson 04264-8 5.95
Music: Advanced Test for the G.R.E., Murphy........ 01471-7 3.95
Philosophy: Advanced Test for the G.R.E., Steiner 01472-5 4.95
Physical Education: Advanced Test for the G.R.E.,
  Rubinger 01609-4 3.95
Physics: Advanced Test for the G.R.E., Bruenn........ 01074-6 6.95
Psychology: Advanced Test for the G.R.E., Morrison .. 04762-3 4.95
Sociology: Advanced Test for the G.R.E., Morrison 04547-7 5.95
Spanish: Advanced Test for the G.R.E., Jassey 01075-4 3.95
Speech: Advanced Test for the G.R.E., Graham 01526-8 3.95

GRADUATE FOREIGN LANGUAGE TESTS

Graduate School Foreign Language Test: French,
  Kretschmer 01461-X 4.95
Graduate School Foreign Language Test: German,
  Goldberg 01460-1 3.95
Graduate School Foreign Language Test: Spanish,
  Hampares & Jassey 01874-7 3.95

PROFESSIONAL ENGINEER EXAMINATIONS

Chemical Engineering, Coren 01256-0 8.00
Civil Engineering Technician....................... 04267-2 10.00
Electrical Engineering Technician 04149-8 10.00
Engineer in Training Examination (EIT), Morrison 04009-2 10.00
Engineering Fundamentals 04273-7 10.00
Fundamentals of Engineering, Home Study Program
  (3 Vols.) 04302-4 45.00
Fundamentals of Engineering (Vol. I), Morrison 04234-6 17.50
Fundamentals of Engineering (Vol. II), Morrison 04240-0 17.50
Fundamentals of Engineering (2 vols.) 04243-5 35.00
Industrial Engineering Technician 04154-4 10.00
Mechanical Engineering, State Board Examination
  Part B, Coren 01258-7 12.00
Mechanical Engineering Technician 04274-5 10.00
Principles and Practice of Electrical
  Engineering Examination, Morrison 04031-9 10.00
Professional Engineer (Civil) State Board
  Examination Review, Packer et al 03637-0 15.00
Professional Engineering Registration: Problems
  and Solutions 04269-9 10.00
Solid Mechanics, Morrison 04409-8 10.00

NATIONAL TEACHER AREA EXAMS

Early Childhood Education: Teaching Area Exam
  for the National Teacher Examination 01637-X 6.95
Education in the Elementary Schools: Teaching Area
  Exam for the National Teacher Examination 01318-4 8.00
English Language and Literature: Teaching Area
  Exam for the National Teacher Examination 01319-2 3.95
Mathematics: Teaching Area Exam for the
  National Teacher Examination 01639-6 6.00
National Teacher Examination 00823-7 6.95

TEACHER LICENSE TEST SERIES

Guidance Counselor—Elementary, Jr. H.S. & H.S. 01207-2 7.00
Teacher of Common Branches 00770-2 6.00
Teacher of Early Childhood, Elementary Schools—
  Kindergarten to Grade 2 .... 00771-0 6.00
Teacher of English, Jr. H.S. & H.S. 00790-7 8.00
Teacher of English as a Second Language, Wellman 04024-6 8.00
Teacher of Fine Arts, Jr. H.S. & H.S. 01037-1 6.00
Teacher of Industrial Arts, Jr. H.S. & H.S. 01307-9 6.00
Teacher of Mathematics, Jr. H.S. & H.S............. 00816-4 8.00
Teacher of Spanish, Jr. H.S. & H.S. 01027-4 7.00

TEACHER PLAN BOOKS

Arco Teacher's Plan Book—Elementary School
  (Grades 1-8) 04029-7 3.00
Arco Teacher's Plan Book—Jr. & Sr. High School
  (Grades 7-12) 04028-9 3.50
Arco Visible Record Books (Looseleaf 6 x 8) 01281-1 6.00
Arco Visible Record Books (Looseleaf 8 x 8) 01280-3 6.25
Cards for Arco Visible Record Books 00761-3 3.00
Leaves for Arco Visible Record Books (8 x 8) .... 07901-0 .85
Leaves for Arco Visible Record Books (6 x 8) .... 07900-2 .85